Praise for *Tío Bernie*

"This book is a true behind the scenes look at the historic Bernie 2020 Latino outreach operation and Chuck's compelling personal story of struggle and redemption."
    -Jeff Weaver, Bernie 2020 Senior Advisor

"Over nearly two decades of studying Latino political outreach and mobilization, I can say without a doubt that the outreach Chuck developed and executed was historic. What set this campaign apart was the union of both scope and depth - the Latino electorate is extremely heterogenous and rapidly growing, and requires a nuanced approach that draws on the shared lived experiences of the population while drawing out the unique facets of Latinx diversity. The Sanders campaign through Chuck's leadership has set a new standard for Latino political mobilization."
    - Victoria M. DeFrancesco Soto, Ph.D
        Assistant Dean at the LBJ School of Public Affairs,
        University of Texas at Austin

"If you only first learned that "tío" means "uncle" in Spanish on February 22, 2020, thank Chuck Rocha."
    -Matthew Butler, Veteran Democratic operative

"Chuck Rocha is the living example of the American dream. This is his moving redemption story, mixed with poignant observations about the current shift in our politics, making this a must read book for everyone."
    -Jon Soltz, Iraq War Veteran and Chairman of VoteVets

"A lot of folks climb the ladder in politics and ignore it behind them, or pull it up altogether. Not Chuck. I think one of the most important roles Chuck Rocha played in 2020 was of political mentor, godfather and champion for a whole slate of young Latinx talent that got their shot in the big leagues because he insisted "the room" needed their voices."
    -Analilia Mejia, Bernie 2020 National Political Director

"Chuck Rocha has been a mentor to so many Latinos inside and outside of Washington. He has fought his own battles so that many of us could have a chance to grow and learn in a way that wasn't available to him when he first got into politics. Every day we are fighting for our seat at the table, and Chuck has been fighting that battle harder and longer than so many of us. In true Latino fashion, Chuck doesn't do anything halfway. If he's in your corner, he'll push you to new heights that you told yourself you weren't ready for. If he's investing in Latino outreach, he'll make sure our community is not just getting the leftover dollars at the end of a campaign. If he's building a trip, he'll make sure we're a part of every event — not just the immigration roundtable. ¡Felicidades, Chuck!"
> -Farah Melendez, Political Director,
> Democratic Attorneys General Association

"Chuck Rocha represents so much of what is great about America- a small town kid from East Texas, with no money and no connections, who overcomes trial and tribulation, goes to Washington and ends up working at the highest levels of American politics. A self described 'Redneck Mexican" who bridges cultural divides, this proud Latino political strategist is supporting a rising generation of Latino leaders across the country who will lead our country for generations to come. His is a story that needs to be told."
> -Scott Bates, Former Secretary of the Commonwealth   of
> Virginia and Secretary of State for Connecticut

"Tío Bernie is a groundbreaking book that is both deeply personal and unapologetically political, because the two are intricately intertwined. Chuck's personal journey gave him the insight and drive needed to pioneer the most successful Latino voter mobilization program to date. The inspiration and lessons found in Tio Bernie are ones no political operative can afford to do without."
> -Maria Cardona, Founder of Latinovations &
> Democratic Strategist

"Everyone talks about the Latino vote but almost no one discusses the urgent need for investment in Latino Civic participation. We are the most underfunded community in our democracy. Chuck is one of the leading voices advancing civic participation by applying structural pressure in Democratic politics. He has been pushing for more diversity and investment as demonstrated by his effective campaigns for Tío Bernie."
> - Hector Sanchez Barba, CEO and Executive Director,
> Mi Familia Vota

TÍO BERNIE

The Inside Story of
How Bernie Sanders Brought Latinos
to The Political Revolution

By Chuck Rocha

STRONG
ARM
PRESS

WASHINGTON D.C.

Cover Design: Lalo Alcaraz
Book Design by Troy N. Miller
Managing Editor: Troy N. Miller

First Edition

Published by Strong Arm Press
www.strongarmpress.com
Washington, DC

ISBN-13: 978-1-947492-52-3

"If you really want to make a friend, go to someone's house and eat with him...the people who give you their food give you their heart."

Cesar Chavez

Contents

Selected Headlines

With help from Latino voters, Bernie Sanders hits the Nevada jackpot

Why Arizona's young Latino voters are fired up about Bernie Sanders and his 'political revolution'

Biden Vs. Sanders: How One Latino Family In Iowa Is Thinking About Tonight's Democratic Caucus

Rep. Jesus 'Chuy' Garcia endorses Bernie Sanders, will rally Latino voters in Nevada

Sanders won big with Latinos in Nevada. The nation's largest minority group could reshape the Democratic race

"That's Called Electability": Diverse Coalition Propels Bernie Sanders to Big Win in Nevada

As Latino clout rises, Sanders leads field in courting them.

Bernie Sanders's Key to Success in Democratic Primary? Organizing in Black & Latinx Communities

Sanders figura como el consentido de los hispanos en Nevada

La maquinaria electoral de Bernie Sanders entre los latinos le impulsa en las primarias de Nevada

Bernie Sanders gets big support from Latino caucusgoers in West Liberty

Buoyed by Latino voters in Nevada, Sanders cements his frontrunner status

WITH NEW HAMPSHIRE BEHIND HIM, SANDERS LOOKS TO NEVADA WORKERS AS VEGAS UNION BOSSES RALLY AGAINST HIM

BERNIE SANDERS'S SECRET TO ATTRACTING LATINO SUPPORT: TALKING TO THEM

HOW YOUNG LATINOS DELIVERED NEVADA TO "TÍO BERNIE"

How Sanders' Outreach Paid Off In Iowa's First Latino Caucus

Sanders' Focus On Latino Voters In California Pays Off

Increased Youth, Latino Voter Turnout Put Sanders Over The Top In California

Latino wave put Bernie Sanders on top in California

Latinos de California lanzan movimiento de apoyo a Bernie

UCLA Data Analysis Says That Bernie Sanders Overwhelmingly Won Support in Iowa's High-Density Latino Caucus Locations

WHAT BERNIE SANDERS IS DOING DIFFERENTLY TO WIN OVER LATINO VOTERS

Inside the Push to Turn Out Latino Voters in Nevada

How Bernie Sanders Dominated in Nevada

Bernie Sanders's Surge Owes a Lot to Voters of Color

What Sanders' Nevada win says about Latino voter turnout

Latinos and Young People Come Through for Sanders in California

Bilingual caucus locations historic first for Latino voters in Iowa

National immigrant rights group endorses Sanders

'Tamales for Tío Bernie': Sanders' outreach to Latino voters pays off

La ola latina puso a Bernie Sanders en primer lugar en California

García, Rodríguez y otros apellidos latinos que donan a los candidatos demócratas. Tienen un favorito: Bernie Sanders

Sanders gana el voto latino en el caucus de Nevada. Domina también entre los jóvenes y los más liberales

'We Went All in.' Inside Bernie Sanders' Plan to Win by Reaching Latino Voters

Bernie Sanders gana popularidad entre los votantes demócratas hispanos, según encuesta de Univision

La campaña de Sanders confía en que el voto hispano lo ayude a ganar el Supermartes en California

Los latinos y condados fronterizos de Texas apoyaron mayoritariamente a Bernie Sanders

Sanders wins Nevada and also trounces competitors with Latino and Hispanic caucus-goers

Latinos were Bernie Sanders's key to victory in Nevada

Sanders bets strong Latino support will carry him to Nevada victory

Sanders's caucus target: Latino voters usually overlooked in mostly white Iowa

The Sanders campaign is counting on Latinos. It seems to be working.

Introduction

This book is a chronicle of the Latino voter outreach program I helped run during Senator Bernie Sanders' 2020 campaign. I go in depth on strategy, budgets, staffing, and the behind the scenes decisions that led to the triumphant public moments and setbacks of the campaign.

I've worked in Democratic politics for 30 years, and for much of that time my passion has been engaging and investing in voters of color, particularly Latino voters. It is my background, the majority of people I know work in the same space and have similar experiences, and it's an embarrassing blind spot in American politics in general, including among Democrats.

But just because our Latino program was historic and successful, and is the focus of this book, doesn't mean other parts of the campaign didn't have success bringing in new voters and engaging key constituencies. There was lots of amazing work done and I want to highlight one area where I think not enough credit is given, and that's to the work done by two incredible black women on the campaign: Senator Nina Turner and national press secretary Briahna Joy Gray.

Nina Turner was the campaign co-chair and her office was

next to mine. There were a lot of trials and tribulations in this campaign and she put her shoulder to the wheel and worked every single day and made sure that a black woman's voice was being heard at the senior level. Not enough is made about how younger black voters were energized by Bernie Sanders and she had a major role in that outreach and in this campaign. I thank God for her presence.

Briahna Gray, who was referred to me, was one of the first hires I was asked to formalize. I was like, "Holy shit, who is this woman?" She's a lawyer, she's brilliant, she can write, and she's got a great communication skill. She would be a perfect national press secretary.

Oh yeah, and she fiercely supports Bernie Sanders with the fire of a thousand suns.

After you get to know her, you learn how much she loves Bernie Sanders, and loves the message and really truly believes in the movement.

But those two black women never get enough credit and I wanted to make sure I'm giving them credit for the amazing work they did from writing policy, to writing ads with me, to making sure that the HBCU tours went off without a hitch. They gave their blood, sweat and tears in South Carolina and across the country. They made sure that black voices were represented at every level of this campaign. Kudos to those two sisters. I would work with them and go to war with them any time, any place.

This book is drawn from my recollection of events, but I also used emails, texts, photos, and documents and presentations on everything from budgets to strategy to confirm things I wrote about.

This book is also not about revealing people's confidences or slamming anyone. I withheld things that would make people look bad, but tried to be as honest as possible, and at times brutally so, in assessing drawbacks from previous campaigns, my own faults, and the bad that had to happen in the past for the good that came from this incredible campaign.

And man, the hardest part was editing myself. I talk a certain way being from where I am from in Texas; I curse and I have been known to be excitable a time or two. But I've kept some sayings I grew up with and things that don't always sound current in the book to teach the first lesson: If you work hard and get some dumb luck along the way, even a semi-literate brown kid from Texas can make it in Washington.

But enough with the small talk . . .

I was sweating like two rats in a wool sock on a summer day. I mean I was stressed.

Once I landed in Las Vegas, I got a call from Jeff Weaver almost immediately. Jeff was my closest confidant on the campaign. He's personally one of my best friends and I respect and admire him so much for giving me the opportunities he has given me, not only on the first campaign, but in this campaign. Jeff Weaver played an integral role in empowering me to get the job done. But because I know him well I could tell Jeff was really concerned.

Jeff wasn't in Nevada. I was the only one in Nevada at the time after the mess that was Iowa and the close win in New Hampshire. I was their eyes and ears: for Jeff, for Senator Sanders, and for Faiz Shakir, our campaign manager.

Jeff probably didn't realize he was doing it but he would end every call, every conversation with, "They have to turn out, Chuck. They have to turn out, Chuck." It just sticks with me today, how uptight that made me feel. It wasn't that Jeff was going to fire me. I knew we'd built something really special with Latino voters. But I remember that feeling of not wanting to let Jeff down, not wanting to let the Senator down.

See, here's the thing. When I tell you Nevada was everything — Nevada was everything. It was to serve as our proof of concept, all the hard work and long hours from staff — door knocking when it was 105 degrees in working-class North Las Vegas, or 22 degrees in Reno in December where an urban cowboy might answer the door.

I was proud of my trademark ju-jitsu tactics I used to reach Latinos in Nevada before any other campaigns or reporters caught a whiff of what we were doing — and all that spending Jeff Weaver had stuck his neck out to OK — but it would all go down the drain if we lost, and I would be on a lonely solo boat ride down to the Florida Keys if I failed.

We saw that the door was cracked open in Iowa, but it would be shut for good if we couldn't pull this out. We had to win and we had to win big with Latinos.

After being on the ground for three days, after I met with the entire field team, I pulled them together for a half-day meeting, two days before early vote was set to start, so they could walk me through their get out the vote — or caucus — plan one more time.

"If there's something we're not doing, I will go get more money to make sure we turn out Latinos," I told them. "We will leave no stone unturned."

After doing a full evaluation of a well thought out plan, I did find a few holes, but that's not a reflection on the staff. They just didn't think that they would have unlimited resources to run a program. In a meeting we figured out that there could be another round of live Spanish calls made every single day, along with Spanish texts to more voters.

So I went and found $200,000 that we took out of the Super Tuesday budget and moved it back over to the Nevada budget, and over a week we pumped out half a million one-on-one Spanish language calls and texts because I was so worried that I'd done all this work and had all these Latinos on board with Bernie Sanders, but they may not show up to vote. So we doubled down.

The last thing I thought of once I was sitting in that meeting was, "Is there anything that anybody can think of that is so absurd that you would never want to bring it up in a meeting because you would be embarrassed to do so?"

They told me that in a general election they might take trucks with big neon signs to drive up and down the strip in Vegas and through the Latino neighborhoods to remind people to vote in our base neighborhoods.

I was like, stop the presses. You're telling me I can get a truck with a big neon sign, light it up, put Bernie's name on it with GOTV messaging in Spanish and play Mexican music in the neighborhoods from dusk till dawn to remind them that early vote starts today?

Long story short, if you want to know how nervous I was, I was so nervous I hastily rented neon trucks for a week and spent $10,000 to play the local Spanish radio station on these trucks in those neighborhoods.

Because after all, they had to turn out. They had to turn out.

Maybe I didn't know it right then, but I was having the time of my goddamn life. I can guarantee you no presidential campaign in history has employed a Mexican redneck as a senior advisor, entrusting them with such a critical part of the campaign. I had come a long way from my farm in East Texas, helping my papaw in the field, and working my way up through my first union job, a journey that would see me criss-cross Texas, land in Pittsburgh, suffer a devastating career setback, pick myself up again, and eventually blossom in Washington where I met a Vermont senator at the Hunan Dynasty Chinese restaurant in 2000, who would change my life forever.

That story, my story, is also the story of how Bernie Sanders looked outside the traditional establishment Washington power structure, elevating and empowering a grateful brown kid from Texas, to prioritize reaching Latino voters. This is the story of the hard work, the gut punches, and dumb luck that led this Mexican Redneck to work for Tío Bernie and how Democrats can work to effectively engage the community in the years to come to create a more equal and progressive America.

But I just really need you to understand one thing. This book isn't about me, not really. And it's not just about Bernie Sanders, though he is the driving force. This is what it's really about. As

his slogan says, "Not me. Us."

PART ONE:

MAKING OF THE MEXICAN REDNECK

Chapter 1

Papaw, Abuela, and the Farm

Bernie Sanders is principled, not overly affectionate, and famously doesn't "tolerate bullshit terribly well," as he told The New York Times editorial board in a viral clip. The same would go for my papaw, my grandfather, who helped turn me into the man I am today.

That story begins in rural East Texas in a small community halfway between Dallas, Texas, and Shreveport, Louisiana. Tyler is the nearest town and we lived 13 miles from the city. So when I say we lived on a small farm in East Texas, what I mean is you had to get in a car and drive for 20 or 30 minutes to go to the grocery store. I'm old enough where I remember riding my bicycle to it, Hopson's grocery store, and scraping and finding pennies and nickels and going in there and buying little pieces of candy for five cents.

I was born and raised by my mother who had me when she was 15 and we were lucky to live in a trailer house, or a mobile home as some would call it, on the little working farm where my grandparents, my mother's family, lived. Onions were a staple on the farm — big, sweet yellow onions — and we also grew corn, potatoes, peaches, okra, tomatoes, peppers, beans and squash. My grandparents sold their produce at the local farmers market in Tyler. Mamaw used that cash to buy Christmas gifts for the family. She called it her Christmas money.

After my father left, my grandfather, Charlie Bussell, who was a World War II veteran, worked on the farm and I was his shadow everywhere he went.

He only had a third-grade education. He fixed trucks. He taught me how to hunt. He taught me how to fish. He taught me how to use tools. He taught me how to put those tools back. It was those early lessons of hard work, tackling projects, and how to figure out things from an old man who didn't look at it through the eyes of a Harvard graduate, but through the eyes of a war veteran, that shaped me.

My granddaddy literally served in World War II and since my mama had me when she was 15, I was a really young kid and my grandparents were super young. My papaw, who went and lied about his age to get into the war, had been deployed to Alaska and ended up being a welder.

I say that to point out that the old man could hardly read and write, but he built every structure on our little farm. He built every barn on that property. He wired every house on that property. He plumbed every one of those properties. And I sat and watched him all the time, figuring things out.

And in a political campaign, a lot of times, you have to figure things out. I think what sets me apart and really what set the Bernie Sanders campaign apart is we didn't always follow the same textbook you were supposed to follow. A lot of that comes from my grandfather, who passed away in 2011. Just telling that story brings tears to my eyes and gratitude to my heart.

My granddaddy was old school. He was a man of very few words. But when he spoke, people listened, and that's how Bernie is. My granddaddy was never the most loving man. He was not somebody who would hug you. He's not somebody who would tell you how much he loved you. In fact, when I think of papaw, I think of burnt leather and Old Spice: he was just gritty, old and wiry. He probably was 5'5, 5'6, maybe weighed 130 pounds sopping wet. He was a small man. But he whooped me and could outwork me all of my life. He was 50 years older than me but when we would pick peas, he could still pick two rows of peas, to my one, and do it way more efficiently.

And you know, as I chased Bernie Sanders around the country and tried to keep up with him at 78, it does remind me of my grandfather. I really believe that people age differently and that age is literally just a number, because I couldn't keep up with my grandfather and I damn sure couldn't keep up with Bernie Sanders.

A lot of times people say that I talk funny. I am this big, over-bearing, very Mexican-looking dude. But since my father left at an early age, I was raised like every other white redneck kid in my neighborhood. I have this accent like my grandfather, this old white guy who came from Kentucky to East Texas and raised three kids, the middle one being my mom, Sandra Bussell.

After watching my mom problem solve, watching her work several jobs, , I think I have a unique perspective on thinking about voters and thinking about messaging to them. I'm trying to reach somebody like my mom, who's working several jobs, who really doesn't care that much about politics. They feel that politics doesn't have a direct effect on their lives, even though it does.

And probably the reason I'm here today is because my mom was so young when I was born, she had my little sister three years later, and my dad left when I was five. So from a very early age, I was the person in charge. I was the one fixing things and tackling challenges.

Looking back as I've gotten older, and having to problem solve through campaigns, especially the Bernie Sanders campaign, I think some of that early childhood trauma and resilience played a big part. I had to go to work when I was 15, and I had to help take care of my sister because my mom worked several jobs.

I remember going with my mom to the YMCA when I was little. She would drop me and my sister off, and I found out some time later, the reason she did that is the YMCA had six-hour swim lessons where they kept you all day and taught you how to swim. So this let my mom go work a second job, and she used the YMCA like free daycare. I also remember leaving that YMCA and stopping by the Smith County community services department where we would get cheese and different things.

Even though my mom didn't know how the government was directly affecting our lives — she was just trying to make it as a single mother, raising two kids — those experiences had a very strong effect on the way I look at politics and look at the making of the Mexican redneck.

I wasn't close with my father Ed Rocha growing up. We grew apart during my teenage years the way that often happens, but reconnected again when he helped get me my first real job. That job — a good union job — not only changed my life, providing healthcare for my newborn son in the short-term, but it also served as my introduction to politics, to running — and winning — campaigns, that would continue me on my path to Bernie Sanders and his movement.

My father met my mother when he was 18 at the West Erwin Baptist Church, where my mother was teaching Sunday school to preschoolers. He was a member of the church because his brother Monty was the choir director. She was 15 at the time and I came along nine months later. My father's family were Mexican-American.

He was one of 15 children of Carmen and Pete Rocha, whose

families had come from Guanajuato, Mexico, and immigrated to East Texas, eventually becoming one of the original Mexican families in Tyler, Texas. Along with the Ramirez family, who owned El Charros restaurant, they were the first two big Mexican families in the area.

Like any self-respecting Latino, I have to mention my grandmother here, Carmen Rocha, the one who bore and had to bear with those 15 kids. Never in my life did I go into abuela's house, when the smell of something cooking wasn't tantalizing you the moment you walked in. It was just the stereotypical abuela household where there was not a place on the wall inside the home where you could put your palm against a piece of sheet rock without one of your fingers touching a picture of one of her 20 or 30 grandchildren at the time.

Since she was always cooking, she always wore a cooking apron. So that's what I remember as a little boy, tugging on her dress, her holding a phone under one arm or her shoulder against her ear, a grandbaby in one arm, and she's literally making tortillas on a hot plate all at the same time.

I remember my nose burning and I remember later in life figuring out why my nose burned when I was at my grandmother's house: it's because she had a molcajete. It's the stone with the stone bowl where she would crush the peppers. And so she'd hit the Molcajetes to make hot sauce and she made tortillas and hot sauce. That may sound stereotypically Mexican but it was beautiful and it happened every single day.

There was a reason when I graduated high school that I weighed 315 pounds. It's because I had a white grandmother who made the best fried chicken in the world, and a Mexican grandmother who fed me flour tortillas with butter and salsa every day. It made a big old brown boy, even bigger. And today it's why I love both of them so much.

But Abuela Rocha's life also tells an age-old story of Latinos and assimilation in America. Her father and mother changed their last name so that their children might have a better chance of finding a job in very-racist East Texas. My grandmother's birth name was Ruiz but was morphed into McRuiz (sounds like McReese) so on job applications, and when you pronounced it, the name appeared to be an Anglo last name. In rural East Texas in the early 1900s it was not cool to be Mexican, which is also why my father's brothers and sisters were encouraged not to speak Spanish. My father actually never spoke Spanish around me. That's why I speak broken Spanish, one of the biggest regrets of my life.

My father and 14 of his siblings were encouraged to assimilate in a big way. It was a different time, in a different place in American history. My father and my grandmother were no less Mexican than the Mexicans in other parts of the country that retained their language, but they were just doing what they had to do to try to protect their children and their family.

When I was five, my dad divorced my mom. We stayed in touch, but really reconnected after high school. By then I had been following in the long tradition, as my mother did, of going to work when I was 15, having several jobs, and helping support the family.

At 19, I got a girl pregnant. It was one of those things that happens in life, and along came my son Charles Allen. It didn't work out with me and his mother. I went to court and was granted full custody. I raised my son by myself since he was six weeks old.

The year was 1990. I'd had Charles, and was working as a milkman delivering milk, not to houses like on the old timey shows, but to convenience stores. I called my dad, and it was probably the single most important thing that happened in my life.

I said, "Look dad, I need insurance because I just had this baby and now I've got custody and I really need a job that's got healthcare."

At the time, my dad was working at Kelly Springfield Tire Plant in Tyler, Texas. To give the scope of how big this place was: It was 24 acres, heated and cooled under roof. It employed 1300 men and women who worked seven days a week, 24 hours a day, on a four different shift rotation of workers.

It was the best job between Dallas and Shreveport. It had the most workers of any place. It had amazing Cadillac healthcare and the highest pay because it was represented at the time by the United Rubber Workers. It also had a strong local union run by a labor icon in East Texas named John Nash.

My father had worked there since he was 20 years old. He worked his way up from being a janitor when he first started there, because he just had a high school education, to the night-time plant superintendent for the entire factory by the time I reached out to him. That meant he ran all of the operations plant-wide for the night shifts.

So when I went to him I knew there were thousands of people in line — always in line — to try to get a job at Kelly, as they called it. When I called my dad, I said, can you get me in? My dad knew I was in a bind, and took me into his house for a while. Charles and I lived with him for a little bit while I was in between places. He sent me to the unemployment office in Tyler, Texas, where you had to fill out an application.

They gave you a test to kind of figure out how smart you were and where you had to do things with your hands. This being 1990, they gave you a board upside down with a bunch of bolts coming through the bottom of it and a bucket full of nuts. One of the tasks was to see how fast you could get all those nuts screwed by hand on all of those bolts.

I later realized what they were testing: it was how your hand-eye coordination was for assembly work, because you're trying to be a day laborer inside a factory with raw material coming in one end and between 30,000 and 40,000 tires a night going out the other end of the plant ready to go on your car.

I took the tests, which meant I could officially apply to work at Kelly. I was working there six weeks later in September of 1990 as a laborer in the Banbury department making the rubber, which was the nastiest department in the factory, in the most heated, toughest part of the job.

This wasn't just important because I got healthcare for Charles, though. I mean that was awesome. I didn't have to worry about my son's healthcare anymore. But what it did is this: it literally put me in position to write this today.

Getting into that factory meant I joined the union, and joining the union meant I got exposed to the Democratic Party and to elections, and to all of the things that I have ended up doing today. It all came because of that one phone call I made to my dad, who wasn't there for me a lot in my youth, but ended up doing the most important thing for me, which changed my life forever.

The cool thing was that I got to spend time with my old man every day. My dad worked the best shifts, but the new guys have to work the worst shifts because it's all based off of seniority. But because of rotations I would overlap with my dad a lot of times, and not just my dad: four of his brothers, and a number of my cousins, also worked in that factory.

The factory was mostly men at the time, almost equally divided between black and white, and less than 1% women. And every Latino that worked at Kelly Springfield Tire Company probably had the last name of Rocha cause it was my dad, his brothers, and my male cousins who all worked there on different shifts. That included my uncle Monty. I was really close to him growing up, and he became a mentor of mine, as I was watching how he worked back there.

Now, let me just pause to note that half of you — plenty of Latinos, and people of color in general — understand where I'm coming from by starting with my personal story and the heat and tire grease, all of it. People like us aren't supposed to get into national politics.

The other half of you think I'm a cocky son of a gun on an ego trip. But let me assure you, this matters. My journey to Bernie Sanders is a unique one, and like the lines on your palm, yours is too. But where we come from and our experiences inform what we bring to campaigns later on. The first election I won was like that, and it's why another Mexican Redneck-ism of mine is "activists aren't born, they're made."

I had the union job and let me tell you, I was like a pig in shit, sitting pretty. But then within six months, the union steward job opened up on my shift, the C shift, in the Banbury. I remember the chief steward came and asked me to take the position.

Now, when you're a union steward in a factory, most of your job is making sure that management is not taking advantage of your brothers and sisters that you work with. There's a contract that the management and the union have to negotiate and it's agreed upon terms that you live by. Union stewards represent workers who may have been wronged contractually and they prove it according to the terminology that's in the agreed upon contract.

The chief steward said none of us kids on the back shift knew what we were doing anyway. He wasn't wrong, and none of us wanted the job, but he wanted me to do it.

I lined up my excuses. I don't really have time. I haven't been here six months. You watched me play high school football, I played with your son, but I ain't that good at reading and writing and don't know much about being a union contractor. I wouldn't know what to do. I'd hate to mess something up.

"Look, I've known your dad for 15 years and he's one of the highly respected people back here," he told me. "He's in management now, he gets along with everybody. We don't have any problems from your old man."

He looked at me and said that if I had this job, and ever ran for office, he was confident I would win. Why? "Because the white folks will vote for you because you sound like them and the black folks will vote for you, because you look like them." Those were the times we lived in back then. I continued to plead my case to Milton Dudley, who we all called Hank.

"Hank, I really don't have a hankering to run for office or run for union steward," I explained. "All I've got to do is load this machine. I'm literally making the most money I've ever made in my life. I've got Cadillac insurance. I now have a defined pension plan and I am living the high life. I just bought a brand new bass boat. This is the best it's going to get."

That's when Hank turned to me and said something that changed my life forever. It's what I talk about from time to time when I ask big audiences, "Do they believe activists are born or activists are made?"

I had told Hank that every 48 seconds my belt moves up and I have to reload the belt with rubber. Then I would sit down, get up, and load the belt again. That's what my job was. You could train a monkey to do what I did and they paid me $22 an hour. I mean it was the best thing ever.

But then Hank dropped the hammer. "Chuck, if you're the union steward and you need to work on union business, the union will bring somebody in on overtime to load the machine for you."

"Sign me up!" I said. "I can do that job." You're telling a 20-year-old kid that you're going to have somebody come do my work and I'm still going to get paid and all I gotta do is be the union steward? Hell to the yeah, I can do that. Oh yeah. That's what started Chuck Rocha's career right there.

But this is what I tell people. It wasn't because I wanted to help my fellow brother or because I had some social mission or something I needed to prove. It was because I could get off work to get somebody else to load the machine. They got overtime, so they're getting time and a half and I'm not having to do nothing and I'm getting paid.

Looking back, I took my union time every Friday night during the last four hours, because where we worked it was really dirty. That meant you had to take a shower before you could get in your car, because you're covered in soot.

So if I took my union time on Friday night, I could be showered on their time and standing in the clock card line at 11:00 PM, ready to clock out immediately when the clock hit 11, so I can be the first one in the club. That was literally my motivation, how soon could I get to the beer joint to drink beer and talk to girls. It was something that seemed so self-serving at the time, but it honestly gave me the opportunity to find my calling in life. It wasn't going to the bars, or chasing girls, but being a really good union steward. It was actually representing workers.

Looking back on it, I was protecting workers. I loved being a union steward and I was really, really good at it. As I got older in life I realized I had always been called to do this job, but I never knew it. It leads to my work with Bernie Sanders, because ever since I was a little boy, I was the one in charge of protecting somebody.

From the time I was young, I was protecting my mama, protecting my sister. I had to be the man of the house. I was 12 years old and I was driving my papaw's tractors and hauling hay. I was the protector. When I got to high school, it continued: I was an all-state right tackle for my football team. I was team captain and I protected the quarterback. I protected everyone. I was the biggest guy on the team at 6'1, 315 pounds. If you were going to mess with us, you were going to mess with me first.

And that led to why I excelled at being a union steward. When I used to work on the factory floor, when somebody would come to me and say they were skipped for overtime because the boss didn't like them and I actually had the power to go get that done for them and get them their money back.

It ties back to what we got hired to do for Bernie and it's why I really love working for him, because everything that we've done is about protecting people. Not protecting the CEOs, or the owners, or anyone else. Bernie, man, he's for the people.

It turned out that Hank wasn't so good at his job. Two years later I ran against him and beat him to become chief steward, which is also the first time that I actually pulled off some Rocha strategy ju-jitsu when it came to an election. It was the first one I ever ran and it was for myself.

The very first time I ever ran for union office, I had to take on a white incumbent who had been in office for 15 years. I was running in an election where just the people in my department could vote for me to represent everybody in the department. Then I would have four junior staffers working for me, one representing each shift.

There were about a hundred guys on day shift and another hundred guys spread out on the back three shifts that are working, second shift, third shift. And so the daylight boys always elected who they wanted to. It was usually some old white guy who looked like all the old white guys on daylight shift, because back then that's where the most seniority was. I was the only Latino besides my uncle Monty in the entire department, so I wasn't going to win this by getting a bunch of Mexicans or Latinos to vote for me. So I started a campaign to mobilize the back three shifts, which were mostly men of color, and largely African-American.

Tío Bernie

I was treating the old guys on the daylight shift like the 1% and talking about it as a time for change, with the back three shifts as the 99%. When we had the election, all the guys in the back showed up for me. I won by nine votes and, at age 22, I became the chief steward in Department 321 in the Banbury. It shocked the entire workplace and the local union, too.

Nobody had ever seen anybody pull off what I had pulled off, but it went back to what Hank had said before: The young white guys liked me because I went to school with them, and the young black guys liked me because I had hung out with them my whole life and we had more in common — so they considered me one of them as well.

So that's how I got elected the very first time. The heart of it was talking about fighting back against the people who had it all, which were those folks on the daylight shift. Everybody wanted to be able to work the daylight shift, cause it started at seven in the morning and you got off at three in the afternoon. That's a cool shift.

Here's what really pissed them off: once I got elected to chief steward, I got what they call super seniority. I got to go to the daylight shift with only three years seniority, while the next least senior person on that shift had 19 years experience. But the joke was on me. They really hated me on daylight shift. I had to work with a whole team of people, none of which had voted for me in the entire election.

Talk about learning Politics 101! That's where I learned how to run campaigns. That's how I learned the intricacies of finding commonality among voters. So when I talk about the lessons that I learned early in my life, that's another one of those lessons that helped me stay steps ahead of your usual establishment consultants out there, who read some manual that they got at Stanford to figure out how to run campaigns.

It all goes back to those oppressively hot summer days when I

37

was in the back of the Banbury staying 20 minutes after my shift to talk to the next shift coming in, to tell them to vote for me because it was time for change. "Vote for Chuck Rocha, Time for Change." I'll never forget that.

Chapter 2

Labor of Love: Leaving Texas and Bernie Stands With Workers

There are moments that stick with you as you mature in life. One is the first time I met the incomparable Ann Richards in 1992, who ran unapologetically for governor as a Democrat in Texas and won.

It was Labor Day, and the local union always hosted the Labor Day parade and picnic at our local union hall. It was a stifling hot day in September. I was sitting on a flatbed trailer, serving as the DJ because me and my sister were singers at the time. I had an amplifier, mixer board, and a microphone, so John Nash (the local union president) always had me do the music and had folks come speak from the flatbed trailer, which I would helpfully inform guests was also mine, and also from the farm.

We were having Ann Richards out to see us in Tyler, Texas, Local 746 and we were all excited. I was there in my cowboy boots and in my jeans that were way too tight for the occasion, wearing a tank top, a big old cowboy hat with hair flowing halfway down my back, and sweat dripping off the side of my face.

As she approached, I ran over and said to John, "The governor's here, the governor's here! What do you want me to do?" He replied, "Well, hell, boy. Get up there and introduce her. You don't need me." So I get up to the microphone: nervous, happy,

39

excited.

At that time I was 22; she had already ran for governor and had already been elected. I helped work on her re-elect as an East Texas volunteer coordinator, putting up yard signs and knocking on doors. But this is the first time I met her. I remember going up to the microphone and shouting, "Welcome ladies and gentlemen, we're honored to have the great governor of the best state in the world, the great state of Texas here with us, Ann Richards!"

I remember everybody going crazy. I walked back to the other end of the trailer to sit down and adjust the microphone. I remember hearing her go as I walked away, "My, my, my, Chuck Rocha, I may just take you back to Austin with me."

Now, that left an impression. It was one of the funniest things that had ever happened to me. I was so stinking embarrassed that the governor had just made those comments about me. It always makes me laugh when I tell the story, but it takes you back to the way campaigns used to work back then.

I loved that period in my life. I had worked on a few campaigns in East Texas by then, but it was time to continue my path: one that would take me from fighting tooth and nail against NAFTA and trade agreements that shipped manufacturing jobs overseas, like the ones my family worked in and cherished — to meeting a senator with white hair from Vermont, first as we rallied labor support, and then later face to face at his favorite Chinese restaurant on Capitol Hill.

After Democrats lost hundreds of seats, and the Republicans and Newt Gingrich swept into power in 1994, AFL-CIO union leadership that had been there forever got moved out for the new wave in 1996. This new wave was Richard Trumka, John Sweeney and Linda Chavez-Thompson.

I was serving my second term as chief steward in my department, where I ran as one of those safe incumbents that I like to give a hard time to. But this was my first entree into being paid staff for a campaign, where the union was going to take me off of my job to go out and actually work on a campaign as a paid campaigner.

At that point my home union, the Rubber Workers, had merged with the United Steelworkers, which is an important part of this story. We merged because we went out on strike against Firestone Bridgestone and they broke the union, which led the Steelworkers to absorb us and help us overcome that strike. The AFL-CIO then asked all the unions to give two or three of their best organizers in each region, to pull them off their job for at least six months to win back the congressional districts we had just lost in 1994.

I was one of three steelworkers out of 30 organizers across the nation who were asked to be part of the campaign called Labor '96. I was the youngest by 15 years, the only Latino, and only one of three people of color.

It led to the first time I got on an airplane, which was to fly from Dallas/Fort Worth to Washington, DC, to be trained how to be an organizer by a young guy named David Boundy, who would both go on to become a great leader in the progressive movement, and teach me so much.

I remember calling and asking, "Where am I supposed to live?" And they replied, "We're going to get you corporate housing," to which I responded, "I gotta live in a corporation?"

That's when they explained that they would pay for a furnished apartment for me. I said, "Hang on, let's recap: You're going to get me an apartment, and you're going to put furniture in it, and you're going to give me money for gas and food every single day?"

Sweet baby Jesus, I thought I'd hit the lottery! I was a single man in Dallas/Fort Worth and they told me I should just go pick an apartment. I remember finding a place up in Arlington with an unbelievable swimming pool and hot tub, where I could spend half my days organizing and the other half laying by that pool. I'll never forget that.

We had literally grown up on this farm that had ponds where the stock would drink their water, which were just little tiny lakes. That's where we swam. I remember getting whooped as a little boy, cause my mamaw thought I was going to get snake-bit because there were all these snakes called water moccasins in the pond.

So getting to go stay in a fancy apartment with furniture that somebody else is paying for and have a swimming pool in it, I thought I'd died and gone to heaven. Plus, I didn't have to work on the factory floor and I'm getting to organize workers? Needless to say, when I was reporting back to David Boundy, when he said jump, I said, "how high, sir?"

David will openly talk about how I was an experiment for them, how they really didn't know what to expect from taking somebody off the shop floor and throwing them into serious campaigning. All of those other folks that were working on the program nationwide were already international staffers — but they wanted to see if somebody from the shop floor, who didn't go to college, who at the time had little vision of the world or economics, could actually do this work.

I ended up proving them right. When my program was over in 1996, it finished ahead of everybody else's — as David would say, by leaps and bounds — based on metrics like how many local union coordinators we could get, how many leaflets we handed out, how many yard signs we could put up, and how many people got involved in those particular races.

For all of the young organizers reading this, I did this without a cell phone and without a laptop until later in the program. I thought I was cool because I had a beeper and a laptop, but I didn't know how to work the damn laptop.

After that, everybody went back to work except for me. David kept me out, and I started working on special elections for the AFL-CIO all over the Southwest. I helped win a number of races, including for Ciro Rodriguez in San Antonio, and lost a lot of elections in New Mexico, before going back to work in the factory for a while.

That's why 1996 was a critical learning experience for me, shaping me as an organizer during a time when political winds were changing. It was also the first time I became aware of Bernie Sanders, before eventually meeting him.

The North American Free Trade Agreement passed despite all of the unions being against it, because a whole bunch of Democrats voted for it after Bill Clinton strong-armed them, but Bernie Sanders wasn't one of them. Back then, we became well aware of the small group of Democrats who had stood steadfast with unions. All of these unions I'd been organizing in Dallas/ Fort Worth were manufacturing unions, and most of them were auto workers, including the General Motors assembly plant I worked out of in Arlington, Texas.

This was a big part of why trade and how it impacts American jobs has always been a huge issue for me. So much so that after the 1996 campaign, I was sent to Washington for a number of months by the union to become a citizen lobbyist for two months against fast track authority (which allows presidents to speed trade deals through Congress despite opposition) for Bill Clinton . This led to my crash course on how Congress and the Senate work.

The first time I actually met Bernie Sanders was during a meeting in his office with a group of union folks trying to make sure we could stop fast track authorization from happening, and he was as on message and focused on the job of protecting workers then as he was during the most recent presidential cycles I worked with him.

For the 1998 elections they expanded the program to include over a hundred people, and put me in charge of four states: Texas, Arizona, New Mexico, and Colorado. As a regional director for Labor '98, I was again on a leave of absence from my local union making 40 hours a week as if I was working on the factory floor. I was still really fortunate. At that point I was in my late-20s and had 35 people working for me in those four states, and I was younger than them by an average of at least almost 20 years.

This was really my first deep-dive into Latino neighborhood politics and the intricacies of the differences between Dallas and Tucson, Santa Fe and Denver. Our crown jewel that cycle was electing Tom Udall to Congress in New Mexico, who ended up being a really good friend of mine.

I got a call from a guy named Jim English. He asked me if I could come to Pittsburgh to talk to the president of the Steelworkers, who at the time was George Becker. All this time doing union work, I'd never done any work for my home union, only the umbrella organization, the AFL-CIO. I'd never worked directly for the Steelworkers.

They had heard I was considering taking a job at the national AFL-CIO. I was, because I was dang sure ready to get out of that factory for good at that point.

So, I flew to Pittsburgh. I stayed downtown, and since there were no cabs, the guy at the front desk said he would get me a hotel car, once he heard it was for the respected Steelworkers, who were a very big deal in Pittsburgh, Pennsylvania, at the time (and in many ways ran the city).

They were still a really big fish in a real small pond there, which was made clear to me when the hotel had a stretch limousine roll up to take me to the headquarters. It was the very first time in my life I had ever been inside a limo, and it was of course the absolute wrong thing to do when headed to a union meeting. But at the moment, for a poor old country boy from East Texas, I thought it was pretty damn cool.

So I get sent up and sit down with Jim English, who ends up being Becker's executive assistant. He's a lawyer and a brilliant man, and would later become my biggest mentor at the Steelworkers. George sat me down and said, "We've been following your career, son, and you're good at these elections."

Then he put me on the spot: "We've been thinking about, do you think you could elect Steelworkers to Congress?

I was like, "Does a bear shit in the woods? Of course I can elect you Steelworkers to Congress. That ain't hard."

I had been out there running races, some of which were for candidates that were not 100% pro-labor. Now I was actually being given the opportunity to help somebody good get elected,

44

who is one of us. In the brashness of my youth, I was thinking, I'd love to do that.

He asked me how I would do it. Looking back, I don't know where the hell I came up with my answer, but it makes a lot of sense. I responded confidently that you would look at congressional districts where there's enough union members alone to elect a union member to Congress. Then you would go in and run a mobilization program on the ground to get those union members out to vote. Almost single-handedly, you would have the union vote put in a union member.

I was pretty sharp for a 28-year-old kid, looking back on it, because I don't know where I came up with that shit. But I remember it like it was yesterday. I went to work, and the first six months I stayed in DC. Then they moved me to Pittsburgh, where I was renting a room from a lady who worked at the Steelworkers. I was making just under $40,000 a year, because that's what I was making at the factory.

I learned through personal experience something that would help me in the future, which is understanding what it's like to be a broke organizer who is passionate about the work they do. One day I came out of my apartment in Squirrel Hill in Pittsburgh and my truck was gone. It was repoed. I had missed a bunch of payments when I was on the road running campaigns.

So when I talk to young staffers about the tolls of running out of money and not having much on the road, I've lived through that personally. It was a very embarrassing and eye-opening experience to get your truck repoed. Looking back on that, it seems really funny now, but at the time it was really sad. We ended up running Steelworkers for Congress in three congressional districts in Tennessee, Indiana and Pennsylvania. We didn't win, but we came close.

I would go on to build out a political program at the Steelworkers that was the envy of the entire labor movement. We installed our own in-house dialer system where we could call Steelworkers at home using a predictive dialer system, which was state of the art at the time, because I didn't want to pay outside vendors to do work we could do in-house. Our rapid response and political mobilization systems were second to none.

I was rising through the ranks and getting to serve on lots of boards. It was really the best job I had up to that point. My son, who I had helped raise back in Texas, moved to Pittsburgh with me and finished high school there.

You know, raising a child when you're still at a young age yourself is not an easy thing to do. I took full custody of my son when he was just three months old. I'll never understand how my mother was able to pull it off, with two children under the age of five, while she was merely 19. I think a lot of it had to do with me and my mother having my mamaw to help us both.

I raised my son, with a lot of help from my mother and my grandmother, and we all did the best job we could. He got to experience life growing up on the farm with three generations of family, and I watched him develop into the same very opinionated, hotheaded young man I myself was growing up on that same farm.

Charles carried on the legacy of our family of having children when he was still a child, but he upped me and my mother by having twins. The literal light in my eyes are those two boys, Rowan and Wyatt Rocha. After high school, Charles kicked around for a while trying to find his way, but ended up moving to Washington for over a year and working at my firm with me and my staff. Looking back on it, those were great years, getting to mentor my son in social justice, and funneling his energy and anger down a righteous path of speaking for the most vulnerable. He was our videographer, and he made some amazing documentaries and videos for our firm.

Charles ended up moving back to Pennsylvania to be with his twin boys, and he is currently a second-year apprentice in the Pittsburgh plumbers union, where he is raising and providing for those boys. I couldn't be prouder.

From day one, Charles has always been a huge Bernie Sanders supporter. He is the embodiment of a young man whose anger drives them to want to see real change in our democracy. Bernie Sanders represents that to my son and young Latinos and young people all over the country. Many times during both campaigns I would channel my son and use him as a focus group with lots of messaging I was testing, swag I was making, or visuals I was using for advertising.

My son now being a father on his own and raising the Rocha boys was a big part of the Bernie campaign that Bernie never knew about. I needed this country to be better than it was on the day that I'll leave it to my boys, and Bernie Sanders was the driving force of how I can make real change. I had a politician who truly was advocating for policies that would directly affect my family and my family members. Every day that I went to that office, when the times were hard and frustrating, I would think about the Rocha boys and my son. I would remind myself why I was doing this work, and why my righteous anger was focused in the right way on making real change for those boys.

Back then with the Steelworkers, there are moments in time that really stand out, some of which would help me with my work for Bernie in 2020, including leading the Latino program. There's also a story we'll get to later that was the opposite — that taught me the hardest of lessons — but also prepared me to fight hard for his political revolution.

But at the turn of the millenium, back before September 11th, I sat down with Bernie in a small, personal setting. It was back when I was the political director of the Steelworkers, and I was able to speak to him more than when I first met him at his office. I remember this meeting in particular, because Bernie loves to remind me about it. We met at Hunan Dynasty on Capitol Hill, where he still likes to order his spareribs and soup to this day (which drives his staff crazy).

I was with union president Leo Gerard. We were lobbying on issues back when Bernie was still in the House, talking about different projects, and building solidarity, and building movements, all the kinds of things that Bernie is really proud of. I'll never forget being in a random Chinese restaurant with this old white-haired guy, with these crazy glasses, from Vermont. Of course, little did I know how much our lives would be intertwined later.

But this was the first time that I ever hung out with him and talked to him at length. So in the beginning of 2019, before he hired me back again to work on this presidential campaign, he said, "Chuck, I remember the first time we met, it was in the Chinese restaurant. You know, I admired your work then and I thought you were really good and I still do. We want you to work for us again."

That's just how he is. He remembered that first meeting. He remembered liking me and that he wanted to work with me. I would've never met Bernie Sanders if my journey didn't take me to the Steelworkers, and for that I'm eternally grateful. But here's my story of why I really remembered Bernie, and will always respect that great man.

Here's what I didn't tell you about going to work as the political director of the union and moving to Pittsburgh only a couple of years later. The factory in East Texas where me and my dad worked and my uncles and all my cousins? They shut that factory down and moved all that production to China.

Not because we didn't make a profit or we were doing a bad job. We made a profit, and a big profit year after year, but they could make more of a profit by making those small radial passenger tires in China.

I ended up working side by side with Bernie Sanders and a whole group of fair trade congressmen to try to stop the "permanent normal trade relations" designation for China, and other trade agreements that literally sent my job, my dad's job, and our families' jobs overseas. I talk about this all around the country when people ask me, "Why do you work for Bernie Sanders?" And I tell them there's lots of issues that I line up with, if not all issues, in absolute agreement with Bernie Sanders.

But the one that stands out, that personally affected me the most, was when these trade agreements took and destroyed the lives and jobs of 1,300 of my friends, my neighbors, and literally my family. They were sent overseas and it still stings to this day. I'll never be able to thank Bernie Sanders for always standing with workers. He always has.

Chapter 3

"I'm Asking You To Print": Hillary Wouldn't Hire Me But Bernie Did

By February 2015, my firm Solidarity Strategies was five years old and humming along as the top Latino firm in Washington, working with all the Latino non-profits and lots of candidates. I was looking to add a presidential campaign as a client. At that point all my friends were telling me that Hillary Clinton was not only going to run, but Democrats were going to clear the field for her.

Well, there was one thing that I knew then, as I do now: no matter who the nominee was going to be, they couldn't get elected without the Latino vote.

I did my due diligence on Hillary Clinton, and found somebody associated with the campaign to figure out how and where to pitch them on hiring a Latino operative as a consultant to help them with Latino outreach. I was really pigeonholing myself a lot in 2015 more than this cycle, where I was the general consultant.

I connected with GMMB, Jim Margolis' mega-firm based out of Georgetown, which was the crème de la crème of all consulting firms at that point. They had done Barack Obama's work on television. They did all the DNC work, all the DCCC work, and they did most of the DSCC work. They did the House, the Senate, and were so large they could wall themselves off internally and do all of the independent expenditures and work for candidates. To top it all off, they had this big book of corporate work as well. So they are a behemoth.

You could tell they built this place to show just how big and badass they really were. I walked into the biggest freaking conference room I had ever seen in my life. It had electric blinds and a screen that came down from the ceiling.

I didn't own many suits back then, so I showed up in cowboy boots, blue jeans, and a sports coat. Where I come from, if you wear the sports coat, that is formal wear: redneck formal. I didn't wear my cowboy hat, because I didn't want to scare the shit out of them. Funny enough, I would take to wearing it during my cable news hits after 2016 and on.

I met with them and my team, showed them our Spanish-language television commercials, our digital work, and our direct mail work. We got good feedback on the pitch. Then, all of a sudden, Jim Margolis himself walked into the meeting, which was a big deal. That's how I knew they weren't just taking the meeting to take the meeting. This was real shit. Jim Margolis was in there listening to my Mexican redneck ass, and everything went really well.

They patted me on the back, showed me around their offices, and that was that. Just to explain, somebody like Chuck Rocha was never going to be the media consultant for Hillary Clinton or any presidential campaign. I probably wasn't going to be the mail consultant.

What happens in almost all presidential campaigns is you have some mega consultant like SKDKnickerbocker, who's currently doing Biden. You have GMMB, who did Barack Obama back in the day. And what they often do is, they subcontract out the Black or brown paid communication to firms who specialize in that.

I feel like that's where you actually lose a lot of the cultural competency, because many of these firms still have a bunch of white boys or interns doing the work. It's not really from the community and by the community. Anyway, I go back to work and I never hear back from them. I never hear anything from the campaign at all. I followed up with my contact at GMMB, and he said he never heard anything really. I would get my answer on what really happened a few months later.

The National Association of Latino Elected and Appointed Officials (NALEO) was holding their yearly conference in Las Vegas in mid-June, and I was at a Latino Victory fundraiser in a hotel suite. It was before Bernie announced, but two months after Clinton announced. All of a sudden I saw one of her senior staffers. We exchanged hellos and I asked if they had heard anything about my pitch. They replied, "Oh, I didn't realize you had pitched."

All of a sudden, it was like a light went off in their head.

The staffer looked at me and said, "You know, I've looked through all of these pitches and there was one group that was head and shoulders above the others and I'm sure now that it was yours. But the only problem was they couldn't pass vetting."

Looking me in the eye, they asked, "Is there a reason you couldn't pass vetting?"

I responded, "Absolutely. I had this problem with the Steelworkers in 2009 and I have a criminal record. It's not anything major, I never served any jail time or anything, but I am a nonviolent convicted felon."

I remember feeling super embarrassed and vulnerable at the time, because I really didn't talk about what happened back then. It had never been heavily reported in any news outlet at that point, so I was really, really shaken by the whole thing. I had worked my butt off to get in the room and to have the best product, but because I couldn't pass vetting, I couldn't work for Hillary Clinton.

Life works in mysterious ways, because that probably ended up being the best thing that could've ever happened to me. Some months later Bernie Sanders would announce his candidacy, but the story of why I couldn't pass vetting led into me working for him. It was a foundational moment not just in my career, but in my life.

It was 2009, shortly after we worked to get Barack Obama elected in 2008, and I'd been at the Steelworkers union for 11 years. My son had grown up. I had raised him all his life, but he had just left the house. I had just turned 40, which was a big milestone for me. But the union was in lots and lots of turmoil.

I was the national political director at the time. I remember we were having to cut salaries because union membership was not where it should be. This had a cascading effect, leading income to be really down for the union. I sat in executive board meetings and knew we were in bad shape. President Leo Gerard and others were making really hard decisions to make sure we could keep our retirement benefits sturdy and keep our work first. So there was a lot of clamping down on expenses, on any kind of extra spending, really.

Looking back on this, it all seems so surreal, but this was probably the first time I really experienced true racism in a workplace. Everybody who worked for me was white and had a college degree, and there was probably some jealousy as well. My secretary and my deputy took it upon themselves to go into my office and take my expense reports and copy them all, and give them to my boss Leo to accuse me of wasting union money, or actually stealing money.

I hadn't done a good job of turning in receipts, and I should have been diligent about that, but I've never stolen anything from that union in my life. I had dedicated my life to it. But it was just the act of them doing that, thinking they could get rid of me so they could be in charge — it wasn't something that really hit home with me until later.

I was super embarrassed that they had done that, and my boss told me he had defended me. I told him I was an open book. I knew that I had done nothing wrong. I certainly had never taken a dollar that wasn't mine, and I prided myself on that. But what the accusation triggered was a six-year audit of my expenses, which is what the Department of Labor does if there's an accusation like that made for any union officer.

We conducted the audit of my expenses ourselves within the Steelworkers Like anybody could, I had made mistakes on my expenses every year. I'd made two or three mistakes every year and, after six years, it was a few thousand dollars.

I was so disheartened by the whole thing. I'd never taken a day of vacation. I dedicated my life to the union, but I had honestly made mistakes on some of the expenses. I still talk about that today when I meet with young people, about the importance of making sure that they really cross their T's and dot their I's when doing their expenses.

I ended up settling with the union, and I realized at that point that I didn't want to be there anymore, if this is what I was going to have to live through. I came to an agreement with the union. We signed a nondisclosure agreement, which is why I don't go into further detail here. I paid them the money that was in question, and then moved to Washington to start the firm I had always wanted to start, but had never had the courage to actually do.

Looking back on it now, I realize that what those folks tried to do to me was the worst and most embarrassing thing that had ever happened to me in my life. But it ended up being the single most important thing that changed my life forever in a positive way. I wouldn't be where I am now if I hadn't flown the Steelworkers' nest and made my own way.

It's important for me to include two final things about this period. I never went to jail. I paid a $2,000 fine and received a year of probation. There was a federal prosecutor in Pittsburgh who thought it would be really a big deal if he could indict a sitting Steelworkers political director, so he took the agreement I made with the Steelworkers and decided that he would go to a federal court and get 18 indictments against me. I only pled guilty to one, for $485.

So yes, I have a $485 felony conviction that you can find if you search on the internet. And people knew about it. A lot of people in the business and my friends circled the wagons and had my back, realizing that I had made an honest mistake and owned it.

I would say to everybody out there, anytime you make a big mistake, you should never lie about it. You should own up to it. That's a big part of redemption. I had worked in a factory. I'd never been to college. I knew little about money or expenses. I'd never really done much credit card work, working out of hotels and the rest. But that's not an excuse.

I still had to own up for a mistake, which led to a non-violent federal felony that I'll have for the rest of my life. There was a dark, uncertain time when I was so worried I was going to lose everything I had over a $500 felony. In the end, it helped me grow as a person, to understand that we can all make mistakes, but then we have to work hard enough to get back from that.

You should be honest with others but, more than anything, you should be honest with yourself.

I learned so much with the Steelworkers, things like running campaigns. I got much better at speaking to big crowds. But what I tell people now who get thrust into positions like these positions, who didn't come up with much money or exposure to the world, is that it can be overwhelming for a young man or a young woman to be put in that spotlight like I was.

In my mind, I was like the star NFL quarterback who had just gotten his first big contract. I got to go where I wanted and do what I wanted. I walked around with my chest puffed out. I really thought I was untouchable. I was a hard worker and really good at my job, but I had really gotten full of myself being at the Steelworkers, where everybody threw accolades at you. I've learned some hard lessons about not letting all that shit go to your head. It made me better at running a business later in life.

That period led to me being able to start a firm that I love, and being able to touch many people's lives, through all the people I've been able to hire, and through pursuing my life's passion. In Washington, Leo Gerard, my former boss and the president of the Steelworkers union — who I had a great relationship with, and who knew the details of what happened — ended up vouching for me and helping me get my first client, which was the Blue Green Alliance. I just started building out my firm from there.

Someone who helped me get back on my feet and make my firm a success was Jon Soltz and VoteVets.org, the oldest clients we have at Solidarity Strategies. But Jon is much more than a client. He is a friend, he is a brother, and he is one of my closest confidants when it comes to everything I've been through the last decade. To be honest, I probably would not be here if he had not been by my side. In the business of politics, true friends are hard to come by. For all of you aspiring political operatives, make sure you surround yourself with a handful of truly trusted friends. They are key to emerging out of your most difficult moments.

Jon was with me through the Steelworkers exit, break ups, each of us losing parents and so many other things. I grew up without a brother. WhileI've always been surrounded by strong women like my grandmother, my mother, and my sister, Jon has always been like the brother I never had. We fight like cats and dogs, but always understand where each other is coming from. We have each other's back.

Anyone who follows my social media knows that Jon and I spend lots of our time on the water fishing. Most of that is done in Everglades National Park with our brother, Steve Friedman. Actually, most of the important decisions I've ever made in my life were made with Jon on that fishing boat in the Everglades. It's one of the few places in the world where we both can find peace.

When Jon got back from his third deployment overseas serving our country in the U.S. Army, he was looking for a place to get away. I told him I had discovered this little village called Islamorada. Early in 2010, he went down and checked it out, and we both came to love it. I instantly appreciated the solitude of being somewhere that was actually quiet. I miss quiet the most living in downtown Washington. After growing up on a farm in the middle of the woods, standing out there on the front of a boat in the Florida bay reminds me of home.

It's OK to fall. It's OK to fail. Eventually we all learn life isn't a straight line, and it damn sure isn't a storybook. That's why I wanted to include this: besides learning from your mistakes, it's very important to know you cannot succeed in this business all alone. You have to have a network of peers and people who have your back, whether it's family, a partner, or true friends like Jon.

There are lots of people in this business that are good at what they do, but they never max out their potential, because they don't prioritize building relationships that help them succeed or get business. It's a not-so-secret way you see white people advance their careers. They have connections and a more affluent network of people who can help them enter the Washington, DC, infrastructure, or whatever professional environment they are trying to break into. The same luxury is just not afforded to many Black or brown young kids coming to DC, looking for their first opportunity. They literally just don't know anyone. It really helps if you have true friends like Jon to help you do this.

That time in my life ties into going to work for Mr. Bernie Sanders.

It was the Friday before Memorial Day weekend, during Spring 2015. I was sitting at my desk when I took a call out of the blue. It was Scott Goodstein, a fellow consultant and a friend. He got to the point and said, "Hey man, are you working for Hillary?" I replied, "No, it just so happens I'm not."

He filled me in on how he was doing some work for Bernie Sanders, who was considering running for president and who I had admired all these years. Scott had built out the campaign website, and wanted to know if I could spend the holiday weekend translating it into Spanish to be ready by Monday.

I told him it's Memorial Day weekend. All my young employees are planning to be out enjoying themselves. If they have to work over the weekend I'm going to charge you double what I would normally charge, but we can get this thing done by Monday.

I tell this story to a lot of young entrepreneurs. I was the CEO and president of a mid-sized political consulting firm in

Washington. Some guy called me and asked me to be the brown guy, and be the Mexican, and translate the website for Bernie Sanders. And I said sure.

Charging Scott's firm double came out to $585. But that first $585, over four years and two cycles, has turned into much more, including memories, prestige and opportunities through Senator Bernie Sanders.

That initial work led Scott to call me and offer to connect me with Jeff Weaver and the Sanders team. He said with my experience working for Barack Obama's campaign, John Edwards and Dick Gephardt, there might be an appetite for someone with my vision. I said, hell to the yeah.

If I knew Bernie was thinking of running, I never would have even tried to work for Hillary Clinton, because he lined up more with my ideological values. I was going to work for Hillary because I thought she'd be the only one running, and it would be great for the firm to actually get to work on a presidential campaign.

I met with Jeff Weaver, who was working out of a townhouse on the Senate side of Capitol Hill, and we just hit it off immediately. He said they needed help building out the states past Iowa and New Hampshire, and really wanted me to help identify talented Black and brown folks that they could hire for some of the upcoming states.

I wrote him three proposals for my team Solidarity Strategies joining the campaign: One was the Pinto proposal at $5,000 a month, the Chevrolet was $10,000 a month and the Cadillac came in at $15,000 a month. This was very little compared to the typical consultants doing this work, but I believed in Bernie and had to start somewhere. We continued having small conversations, but there were a lot of demands on Jeff's time, which I understood.

What happened next would accelerate everything.

By then, June had come around and every progressive was at the Netroots Nation conference in Phoenix. This was the convention where Black Lives Matter protesters took the podium from Bernie Sanders, and he backed away. He let them have their space and talk about the issues they wanted to give a larger platform to.

It was embarrassing for the campaign and for the Senator, and a real pivotal turning point in the campaign at that time in 2015. I remember being in the crowd, and how bad I felt for Senator Sanders during the whole process.

But context is super important here. Progressives and Democrats writ large had not done a good enough job centering and elevating the voices of Black people. So that's why Black activists and organizations, including many Black women leaders, decided to make that space for themselves. Sure, it was a little uncomfortable for organizers and attendees, but if there's anything we've seen now in 2020, it's that Americans needed to be made uncomfortable. It's no surprise then that leaders like one of the co-founders of Black Lives Matter, Patrisse Cullors, were at Netroots back then, and continue to lead now.

Soon after Netroots, I got a call from Jeff. He said we should move on one of my proposals (the smallest one), but I was excited. He said I could start by helping identify Latinos and African-Americans we could hire.

Since we were coming to our agreement then and there, I felt at that point it was my duty, because of what happened with Clinton's campaign, to tell Jeff, "Look, you need to know about this because I don't want to do anything to hurt the Senator."

I told him that what had happened with me was a Google search away, and that he could find something about the Steelworkers political director being indicted for embezzlement. I walked him through all of it.

Jeff heard me out, but then turned to me and said, "Oh, we know about this. We knew about this the first time we talked to you." Stunned, I replied, "Have you talked to the Senator?" He said of course he had.

What's more, Bernie Sanders had responded, "How long

are you supposed to pay for a mistake that you made back then, that you've already paid for? Are you supposed to pay for this the rest of your life?"

The message from them was that I was past those troubles. Everybody that they had talked to, including Larry Cohen (their liaison to organized labor), had all said I was the best to do this work — so they wanted to hire me.

This was no small gesture to me, and involved a bit of calculated risk. In fact, early the next year, to hurt the Senator, someone would drop some opposition research about my hire in a story online, and Jeff Weaver would again have my back.

"It's not politically sensitive at all," Weaver told the reporter. "I'm not politically afraid of this story at all. Please, I'm asking you to print."

When I was back sitting with Jeff, I remember choking back tears. I was thinking that I would work for Bernie Sanders for the rest of my life, because he literally had my back and was willing to give me an opportunity that others wouldn't at the time.

I mentioned the Hillary Clinton campaign, but she wasn't the only one. During that time in my life I had lost a lot of work over what had happened in Pittsburgh, but I had also kept a lot of clients. I kept more clients than I lost, thank God. But it was at that point in time where I really, really came to admire Jeff Weaver, and learn that Bernie Sanders was a man of his word, who would have my back, and so I had to have his.

Chapter 4

The Seeds of 2020, Planted in 2016

To understand what the Sanders campaign did in 2020, you have to begin in 2016. There are two common misconceptions. First off, what people know as the progressive movement Senator Sanders breathed life into, and how important it is to the Democratic Party and the country moving forward. Where we are now is not where we were then, not by a longshot.

Secondly, if you bring yourself back to 2016, you think about the powerful insurgent campaign, the $27 average donations and the mammoth grassroots fundraising. All of that is true. But that didn't start at the beginning. Early on, we had a shoestring budget, and staffing the campaign was a much different story.

After Jeff Weaver and the senator literally changed my life by taking me in and letting me be a consultant for the campaign, I started immediately looking for brown and Black folks to hire, calling and meeting with everybody that I knew. But in 2015, it was hard in DC to find experienced people who would work for Bernie Sanders. The top people from the establishment wing of the Democratic Party were already working for Hillary Clinton. They had many of the top consultants, for example, and some of the best staff.

So I would call somebody and say, "Hey, I'm Chuck Rocha, with Solidarity Strategies, and I'm calling on behalf of Senator Bernie Sanders to see if you'd be interested in being the state director in Nevada?" If they were really good, they probably were already working for Hillary at some level.

The other half were scared to go to work for me and Bernie Sanders because they were scared that Clinton-world would punish them if they went to work for us. If they were younger, talented folks who didn't have a ton of experience, they were afraid that if they went to work for us, they would be blackballed by the party, and never get a job at the DNC or with the super PACs.

Later, people would tell me they wanted to work for Bernie, but feared retaliation. So it was really a challenge. It was a stark difference from 2020, when I was probably getting 30 or 40 resumes a day from people who said they would love to work for Bernie.

The process did infuse a certain spirit into the 2016 campaign. For example, I'm kind of a misfit. I speak like an old white man from the South, but I'm really brown and look very much Chicano when you see me. I know what it's like to have a rocky past or not be the perfectly imagined fit for a role. So I knew there were people that deserved a chance. Jeff and Bernie gave me a chance, so I wanted to go find people who needed a chance. We found some decent folks; not all of them were perfect. Many worked out, and some of them didn't. That was my job at the time, and I was proud to do it. But eventually, I had an idea, so I sat down with Jeff.

At this point in July 2015, I'd never pitched Bernie Sanders to do his TV, his mail, his radio, to run a Latino program + nothing like that. I was a consultant, tasked with expanding the pool of applicants to help hire some folks who weren't white men. But I told Jeff the campaign was making all of this literature and shipping it all over the country, in a sort of ad hoc way. They were spending a lot of money on transporting it, designing it, and mailing it.

So I said, my expertise is in direct mail and I've done a

little bit of an analysis. Because I was a union mail consultant, I already had union print shops in every single state. I estimated that if he let me do the literature and centralize it through my firm, we could probably save the campaign $1 million over an eight-month period. Weaver said, "That sounds good to me."

Suddenly, I was doing all the literature for the Bernie Sanders campaign, outside of Iowa and New Hampshire, where there was already someone in place. For all of the other states, I centralized all the mail, and developed a process where Jeff would write the six to 10 literature pieces that I knew we would need in every state.

For example, you need a biography piece in every state, an African-American piece in every state, a Spanish-language piece in every state, or something aimed at college students. So we did all of that ahead of time, and that was the process we used to send out millions and millions of pieces of literature.

That process — putting your head down and working hard, but knowing when it's the right time to seize the opportunity and speak up with constructive ideas — is a good one for young operatives to understand, and it led to Weaver asking me if I wanted to be the mail consultant for Nevada. He thought it'd be good if he had a Latino-owned firm do the mail in the state, since a lot of it was probably going to be bilingual at some level.

That's how I got to be one of four mail consultants on a major presidential campaign. But this was still early. When we started in 2015, nobody thought we were going to raise any money, so nobody knew if there'd be any money to do any mail. Everybody thinks Bernie Sanders was always raising tens of millions of dollars every week, but that didn't start in the campaign until the Fall, when folks woke up and decided we had a chance to win.

As Jeff Weaver wrote in his book How Bernie Won, the original budget that was basically scrawled on the back of a napkin was for $30 million. Didn't none of us think we could actually get $30 million, but we were going to give them hell and give our best effort. So it's important to keep in mind that a lot of the building blocks of the campaign came on a shoestring budget.

We didn't even have an office. We were in a little townhouse in Washington, DC, and eventually the Burlington office.

Then one day, I got a call from Weaver, who said my old friends at the AFL-CIO were going to have a meeting in a month to determine their endorsement. Jeff reminded me of what we all know: That Bernie Sanders had been a stalwart advocate for labor and collective bargaining his entire life. We needed to stop this endorsement if it wasn't going to go our way. He asked if I had some ideas. I said yes: I have lots of ideas.

He filled me in on how Larry Cohen, who had just retired as the president of the Communications Workers of America, was working on it, but he couldn't do it all on his own. Larry's union was also a client of mine for a number of years when I first started my firm, Solidarity Strategies. What's more, I had a close relationship with Larry and one of his deputies, Yvette Herrera, who is a great friend and was one of my mentors.

But Larry can also be challenging. He's very excitable, high-strung, and he brings a lot of energy to the room, but he also brings a lot of chaos. If Jeff wanted me to work with former President Cohen, I was more than willing to do it, because I loved Larry, but I was already doing the work I was hired for and had picked up other mail work. For the first time, I asked Jeff for a bigger retainer — up from $5,000 a month to $7,500 — and he didn't even flinch.

For some consultants that might not be a lot of money, but I was proud to get to this point, right? My papaw used to say "pigs get fat and hogs get slaughtered." There was no need to be a hog when they were putting enough food out for the pig, and I was getting to work on a campaign I believed in so deeply.

We ended up stopping the union's endorsement. Now I was putting together the labor strategy and mail strategy. My role in the campaign continued to grow. They liked me, saw that I was working hard, keeping my head down, and that I was no trouble. On the contrary, I was an asset. So they gave me more and more and more to do.

It's been documented that there were a lot of problems

with the campaign in its early days, mainly because of the exponential growth all at one time. I wasn't in the headquarters. I worked from my firm's office, so I never saw anything negative.

I just did whatever Jeff needed me to get done. I remember he started to come to me to ask me questions about Latino things. That led to the first time I saw firsthand that Senator Sanders could move a Latino audience — and in this particular instance, maybe a group that started the day with a bit of skepticism, but ended up loving him. It would prove to be something I filed away for later.

It was July 2015, the week after Independence Day. Bernie Sanders was in Kansas City for the National Council of La Raza (NCLR) convention, the storied Latino civil rights and advocacy organization, now known as UnidosUS. They were a client of mine at the time, and it was very important for me that Bernie do well.

Senator Sanders was a staunch ally of working people, who absolutely never wavered, but he hadn't always talked about immigration the way that some on the left would have liked him to talk about immigration. In fact, just a month before speaking to NALEO's group of Latino elected and appointed officials, some had felt that they wanted him to be stronger in speaking about immigration reform.

So I really wanted him to make a strong statement, to knock it out of the park in front of these Latinos at NCLR. The audience included grassroots folks, but also some bigwigs from around the country who maybe weren't quite sure what to make of the senator from Vermont just yet. Jeff did all the writing back in those early days, and he wrote one of the best speeches I've had the pleasure to hear.

We were dealing with the ongoing issue of the deportations of the Obama-Biden administration, and the continued fallout within the community from those decisions. The speech ended up being so good that we used it in our Spanish-language television commercials. Back during the first campaign I didn't make the Spanish ads; they were produced through the firm Devine Mulvey Longabaugh. I would translate them, and I would give them production ideas, but I wasn't making them like I did in 2020 with the help of the team.

The speech had important concepts that Senator Sanders would continue to harp on in 2016 and in 2020. Of Donald Trump, he talked about how he was trying to divide the nation with old racist ideas, and spoke about his own history losing family in the Holocaust. He also explained immigration in terms the people in that audience knew all too well, remarking that, "Without these folks, it is likely that our agricultural system would collapse." It wasn't a one time only thing, either. Just weeks earlier at NALEO, he had said some people wanted to send unaccompanied minors back like packages marked "return to sender," which struck a chord with me and others in attendance.

But Unidos was the first time I saw him interact with a Latino audience that really lost their shit in a good way when they heard him, including standing ovations, and our trademark whooping and hollering. He had always had crazy, lefty Mexicans like me who loved him. But this was the establishment Latino class at NCLR and grassroots folks from around the country, and he got a rousing response.

Jeff wanted to work off of that momentum, and another moment from that speech provided the opportunity. Senator Sanders in 2007 had intervened to stop the horrendous exploitation in Immokalee, Florida, where undocumented workers grow tomatoes. The U.S. attorney had indicted people literally for slavery, for workers being forced to work against their will. Bernie talked about how giving attention to an issue far from Vermont led to better wages, working conditions, and housing for workers. He just saw a grave injustice, and acted. So we told that story in a two-minute documentary television commercial on Univision, which was groundbreaking.

We had more of an inkling now that Latinos liked Bernie Sanders when they got to know him, when they learned his family's story, and when he talked about the issues he cared about (beyond his stump speech) that also animate the community. So in the Fall of 2015, I asked Jeff if we could run a Latino experiment in Nevada. We had just started to raise real money, so I proposed using my call centers to call Latinos in Nevada and ask them who they're going to vote for: Bernie Sanders or Hillary Clinton. Then I wanted him to let me send them three pieces of bilingual mail after the calls, and put up radio commercials for two weeks. To top it all off, I wanted Jeff to send the senator out there, in the middle of when the mail and the radio was going to hit. Finally, I wanted to call them again when all of this was done, to see if Latino voters were moveable or completely behind Clinton.

This is what I call a Mexican Redneck poll. It didn't involve a political scientist, but I had just figured out a strategy that didn't cost that much money and didn't have to involve a lot of other vendors. It was a test to see where we stood with Latinos. I knew if I could move them, then I could get more money to do more communication. I called 500 Latinos with my call centers and Hillary, of course, was beating us by 15 points. But Spanish speakers, who you would have thought would be solidly in her corner, were more with us than expected.

I never could figure out exactly why, but of course I have some ideas that are to come. After we did the mail, the radio, and Bernie went out there for his first trip, the numbers moved exponentially. Once Latinos found out who he was and saw his message, they moved in our direction in dramatic fashion. We still didn't catch up to Hillary, but we got close. Even at that point, I thought that could give us a fighting shot.

We ended up not doing anywhere near the program that we ran in 2020, but I took what we learned in 2016 with me. I used it to know how to do it better four years later. Even though the 2016 campaign fell short, I want to make it clear that so many staffers did a great job, including with Latino outreach.

The resources in 2016 were not comparable to what I was working with in 2020, and I was empowered in a much different way in the later campaign. I think the work they did in 2016 truly laid the groundwork for what we were able to accomplish in 2020, though. A lot of folks say, what was the biggest difference? It wasn't me or my great ideas. Beyond the groundwork that was laid, there were structural things. This includes how things were siloed. I pushed for structural changes to make sure that everything was integrated in 2020, which we'll get into.

PART TWO:

JOINING
THE
REVOLUTION

Chapter 5

Bernie Goes Rogue:
On the Road with Bernie as He
Decides to Run in 2020

It is not broadly known that the Latino vote was not only a key part of the 2018 blue wave that took back the House, but also served as a critical pillar of Bernie Sanders' thinking as he came to the decision on whether he would run in 2020. That process includes an unforgettable story of staffers scrambling, as Senator Sanders of Vermont strolled through the barrio on the road from Nogales to Tucson in arid Arizona — with me chasing after him in cowboy boots. But let's begin with January 2018.

It was reported in the media, so I won't get into this too deeply, but Bernie Sanders held a meeting with top lieutenants early in 2018. This was during a time when he truly didn't know if he would run in 2020. The meeting also included decisions on how the senator would devote his time and energy in the run up to the midterm elections.

This would be the first election since Donald Trump was elected. There was real excitement in the Democratic Party and the progressive movement. People had crazy ideas like being able to take back the House, which seemed like a longshot with so few congressional districts in play.

As I said, Jeff Weaver had written a book after 2016. He was looking forward to returning to the comic book store he owns and runs in Virginia. He got pulled back into the fray because he's so damn loyal to Bernie Sanders. Ari Rabin-Havt, who would end up being the deputy campaign manager for the senator, is a friend of mine. I know his family. He was on SiriusXM radio for a number of years, and I would go on his show once a week.

So hearing from Ari, or getting invited to his house, wasn't unusual, but hearing that Jeff and a small number of advisors to the senator were going to be there to give him our thoughts on Bernie running for president? That was definitely memorable.

I could tell you everything that happened in that meeting, but the final decision is the only thing that really matters. I could do it anyway, to make myself look really cool. But that's not interesting. Here's what is. When you care about and prioritize Latino outreach, or any kind of important outreach to brown and Black folks, you come up with a lot of terms for what was happening here — or rather, usually doesn't happen.

My friend Cristóbal Alex, who I worked closely with for many years when he ran Latino Victory Project before he joined the Biden campaign as a senior advisor, has a term for it. He says if you're not at the table, you're on the menu. Unfortunately, brown and Black folks have a lot of different names for this, which establishment operatives should take note of. But that's what was happening here. I was at the table. I was in the room. That's the first part of effectively reaching Latinos, and there's a lot more to it, but if you're not in the room, you're not impacting decisions on everything from staffing to spending. Unfortunately, that's the case with Latino investment and engagement much too often.

So sure: I was proud, I was nervous, I was excited. I was all of those things. I remember I showed up early. For anybody who's known me for more than two minutes, you know that I'm early for everything. My mama always taught me, we may not have much money, but you can show up on time. So I'm just a stickler about being on time. Matter of fact, I always thought that my first book would be called "Advice to the American People: Show up on time, be nice, and chew with your mouth closed." But

I like Tío Bernie better.

Anyway, I was the first one there. The others there were Jeff; Tim Tagaris, our digital genius; Ben Tulchin, our pollster; Arianna Jones; Senator Nina Turner; Ben Jealous; and Mark Longabaugh and Julian Mulvey, from DML. Jane Sanders — along with RoseAnn DeMoro, former head of the National Nurses United — joined us by phone as well. We gave our opinions, and sketched out what it would look like if we were going to do this again. The senator, to his credit, just sat and listened. Bernie is honest to a fault. He really had no idea if he was going to do this or not. When he said he wouldn't jump in if somebody else was running that he thought could win, that was true. He always said that in private.

The biggest takeaway was, of course, where we ended up. Bernie decided he would travel around the country and help elect as many Democrats as we could in 2018. We all agreed that this would be the bedrock of the strategy in 2018. If he decided he wanted to run for president, he needed to get out there and work his butt off to help Democrats get elected.

Now's the time to admit I had been a staunch hater of the DCCC, which you may know if you've heard me over the years or ventured over to my Facebook wall. The reason why? The whole time I'd been a consultant, they always had the same group of consultants that always did all the work over there. The senior leadership at the committee would always get a job at those consulting firms, or at a consulting firm that would then end up getting a contract with the DCCC. So it was a very closed circle over there, one that none of us brown and Black consultants could break into. It was a constant tension point for me.

I'm already outspoken and hotheaded, so I didn't take any shit from none of them. I called them out every single day about it. But Congressman Ben Ray Luján really, really changed things at the DCCC when he took over, prioritizing the Latino community. This also positioned me exactly where I needed to be to run the program for Bernie Sanders in 2020.

Early on, Ben Ray brought in one of his right hand men, Dan Sena. I had known him for 20 years. I had organized with Dan in the Southwest during our twenties in New Mexico and in other places, along with a whole crew of guys who are now big shots in the political world from Bubba Nunnery to Sean Sinclair. We were this crew of 20-year-olds just traveling around the country, working on one special election after another, so you become this tight-knit family. So Dan Sena was the executive director of the DCCC? You have a Latino chair and a Latino running it? If I was ever going to have a chance, it was going to be then. So I sat down with Dan. He said, "What should we do? What can we do differently and how can we prove we're going to do this differently?"

In the moment, I played it cool. But in my head, it was a lot like when the clouds part and the sun shines down in a movie. I told Dan — and this is going to sound familiar — that you have to talk to people of color, and especially Latinos, early. You need to talk to them at every single level, and make sure that you're running a program targeted directly to people of color. "If you do that, I think you can actually win all of these seats you want to win back," I said.

Dan sent out a request for proposals to consultants, and was calling the program "The Year of Engagement," which meant talking to Latinos and Black voters in the year before the election. He asked me to write a plan for DCCC. That plan would provide valuable lessons for Bernie Sanders 2020.

I am not a prolific writer, but I wrote a 27-page plan that weekend. Writing isn't my favorite thing in the world. I did this book because the story needs to be told. Before this, the longest thing I'd ever written was that 27-page memo to Chairman Ben Ray Luján and Dan Sena.

It said we should identify all the districts where the people of color make up a substantial part of the districts — I think it was over 15% — and start doing focus groups and polling early in these districts, along with mail, digital, radio and Spanish-language television strategies. Long story short, I got that contract. Plus, they gave me another one to do all the phone communications for all of their races. By the end of the campaign, we won 32 of the 49 races we worked on. We helped fuel the year of engagement dedicated to talking to brown and Black voters, and helped trigger the blue wave that made Nancy Pelosi Speaker in 2018.

I took a lot of that institutional knowledge, and implemented it with Senator Sanders' campaign. It was proof of concept of what could really happen if you invested in the correct way, even though the DCCC didn't invest as much as our campaign did in 2020, which we'll get to. But those focus groups on what Latinos were thinking in places like Miami, Orange County and New Mexico were invaluable.

The DCCC focus groups were run by Latino Decisions, including my good friend Albert Morales, a hilarious Texas Mexican who has forgotten more about Democratic politics than most people will ever know, and Matt Barreto, an incredible pollster and political scientist who does great work surveying attitudes in the community, which affects policy change and gets Democrats in line when that's needed.

The focus groups were of Latino drop-off voters, or voters that don't take part in every election. Sitting through those focus groups really helped me figure out the messaging for Bernie Sanders prior to me ever having any polling in any of the districts we were working in. I would end up discussing one of those takeaways with Bernie on the road, later that year in Arizona.

True to the plan, Bernie Sanders hit the road with Ari in the Fall of 2018, holding one big rally after another to get people excited towards the end of the cycle. But there was also a discussion about where he should travel, since he can't be everywhere and campaign for everybody.

Obviously, he went to places where he could make a major impact, but also places where we believed there was some untapped potential for support for the senator, if he chose to run. Knowing that there was room to grow with Latino voters, I was invited along as his travels took him through the southwest to Arizona. There, we took part in a border tour in late October. We talked about Donald Trump's border wall with community activists at an event I put together in Nogales.

On the way down there, between Tucson and Nogales, there isn't a lot to see on that great road. As we drove, Bernie said he wanted something to eat. After being stuck in Washington, DC, for so long, my only demand was that we get Mexican food if we're in Arizona. None of this Waffle House shit, please. To that, Bernie replied simply, "Chuck, I love the Mexican food. We should do the Mexican food."

So we found a Mexican restaurant. It was called Manuel's Mexican Food. It was like 9:30 pm at night, the restaurant was probably getting ready to close up, and we showed up at the front door rolling 20 people deep. It wasn't because Bernie usually travels with that many people, but because we had a lot of people who were going to be involved in the border education event.

This was just the latest example of witnessing something and thinking to myself, "Holy shit, Mexicans really do love Bernie Sanders." I mean, this place lost their everloving mind. It was full of Latinos, full of Mexican-Americans, in their boots and cowboy hats just like me. And Bernie just rolled up with his posse to ask for a table.

The owner came out. They rolled out the red carpet, even though we probably just fucked up their plan to close. Bernie got the enchiladas, we ate, and then he wanted to talk to the workers in the back of the restaurant, like he always does. We talked to the cooks and the waitstaff. He took pictures with the staff, and people were just falling over themselves, beaming with happiness. By now it was just a constant reminder that there is something fundamentally special about the connection with Latinos and this man.

We had a great round table and rally the next day for David Garcia, who was running for governor. We also met with LUCHA, an incredible community organization run by two of my friends, Tomás Robles and Alex Gomez. It included a special interactive meeting with organizers on the ground, who talked to Bernie about the challenges of door knocking and grassroots organizing.

As we headed back to Tucson the next day, it was time to eat again. We stopped at another roadside Mexican restaurant, this time in the barrio, seemingly in the middle of nowhere. Now, you already know my story and where I come from: I love stuff like this. Nico's Mexican Food was a taco joint, one of those no frills places that have the best fucking food, bar none. Some of the tables didn't have tops. There was limited seating, bolted to the ground. It was great.

(A bit of Mexican food advice from someone who knows: If you go into a strip mall and find the Mexican restaurant that's the furthest off the road, that's the cheapest rent. Those are the places we like to get and they have the best food. Just so you know.)

Anyway, Bernie gave his order to someone and we all took turns going inside to get our food in a neighborhood teeming with energy, dogs running, babies in diapers hollering and folks going back and forth with each other.

And that's when Arianna Jones, who would be Deputy Campaign Manager in 2020, noticed Bernie was gone. So she grabbed me by the shirt, and told me Bernie had gone rogue. "You gotta go get him, Chuck," she said.

What people don't know is that Bernie likes to go for walks. He's one of the most well-known people in America, he's a U.S. Senator, and there are a lot of demands on his time, especially during a presidential campaign. So sometimes, he just likes to unwind and go for a walk. The other thing he loves is just talking with regular people in unscripted environments.

I didn't find out it was a common occurrence until later. So it was surreal and hilarious to see Bernie just walking in the middle of the hood all alone, in an area none of us knew. So I jogged over in my cowboy boots to walk beside him. He didn't have a care in the fucking world. He was just bebopping down the sidewalk, enjoying his stroll through the barrio, and chatting with people, as neighbors peeked through their blinds thinking, "Holy shit, that looks like Bernie Sanders, but what would he be doing here?"

He ended up safely making it back, of course, but I will always remember the day Bernie went rogue.

Later, in the van together, we sort of informally debriefed after all these moving meetings about the border wall. We had heard from lots of local activists who talked about how the border wall was going to negatively affect their life if they continue to build the stupid thing.

Bernie, who usually gets on his iPad when he's traveling like that because he's a prolific reader, was instead talking about all the Latinos he met that made an impression on him and the reception he got from the workers in the back. He was also talking about the people during his walk, and the activists who came up to him with the look of respect you only get when you see them, recognize their humanity and their struggle, their "lucha."

"Why do people always say that Latinos don't vote?" Bernie asked me, adding a question for good measure about what needs to happen to get Latinos engaged to vote.

So no biggie. Just the (multi) million dollar question that gets asked every cycle. Here I had the opportunity to have this critical conversation with Senator Sanders, who was considering running for president. As we rolled down the interstate, we talked for an hour about engaging and investing in the community in a serious way. This was the first of my conversations talking with Bernie about the Latino vote.

My ideas were about how you could engage the community. I had learned a lot from sitting in on the focus groups earlier in the year with Latino Decisions for the DCCC. The primary takeaway was that maybe these voters couldn't name their congressperson, but they could repeatedly tell us that healthcare was their number one issue, a driving force in their lives. I think that was one of the first times Senator Sanders connected the dots on how the core issues that were central to his politics, like Medicare for All and healthcare costs, also animated the Latino community.

The importance of that trip proved to be the latest confirmation of a maxim we Latinos know all too well: Thank God for Mexican food.

Chapter 6

If Your Eyes Glaze Over When You Hear Diversity and Hiring, You're Doing It Wrong (Building the Bernie 2020 Multiracial Foundation)

We had four or five meetings leading up to November with the same group that had met at Ari's house in January. We talked about what different parts of the campaign would look like, which accelerated after the November midterm elections. Right out of the gate, Andrew Yang announced for president. Elizabeth Warren would follow in December. We knew that with the New Year, a whole slew of major candidates would enter the race.

There was a lot of pressure on Bernie to announce early, but he hadn't made up his mind. A lot of us knew we had to be prepared if and when he did so. The earlier he announced, the sooner we could start raising money and putting together the infrastructure for a long, drawn-out battle with multiple candidates. One of the first jobs Jeff Weaver gave me, before we even had an apparatus to pay me, was to identify prospective staffers to hire. By now you know our most clear and present priority was helping to make Bernie Sanders' 2020 campaign one of the most diverse in American history.

When I left the Steelworkers in 2009 and started my firm

in January of 2010, I knew that I wanted to take what I had learned at the union and combine it with an urgent need that I identified doing national politics at that point for 20 years.

No matter what room I was ever in, including some of the most powerful rooms in American politics — from AFL-CIO board meetings, to presidential campaign meetings with advisors for John Edwards or Dick Gephardt — I was always the only person of color in that room. There was never a Black or brown person, and there was rarely ever a woman in the room. I knew I had an opportunity to make changing that my life's work. That's the reason I started my firm, Solidarity Strategies.

Sure, I could have called it Chuck Rocha, Inc., or something else terrible of that nature, but it just wasn't about me. This is why the way I think about politics is a lot like the way Bernie Sanders thinks about it. There's a reason his motto is "Not me, us." The firm was about what I could do to create more Chuck Rochas, but at a younger age. So I was very intentional about the way I built out my firm, one that would later become the largest Latino-owned and operated national political consulting firm in the country.

In the decade I ran Solidarity Strategies before joining Bernie Sanders' team as a senior advisor, we had almost a hundred people come through the firm. We figured out a way to have a political consulting firm double as an incubator for young brown and Black kids who may not have otherwise had a viable way of entering the Beltway bubble.

Steve Phillips, a smart Democratic donor who understands the value of diversity just as much as I do, and wrote a book called "Brown Is The New White," asked me once how I defined success. I told him I hoped my legacy would be not about how many campaigns I won, but how many people's lives we touched through the firm. I hoped they could go on to have incredible political careers and even start their own firms at some point, which just happened recently with my former right-hand and brilliant operative in her own right, Vanessa Moyonero. Many employees from my firm also went to work for the Bernie Sanders campaign throughout the years. That's a point of pride for me, and another way diversity and inclusion fueled the campaign.

I used almost the identical approach as I used over the last decade to help build out Senator Sanders' presidential campaign, with an intentional focus towards building up and giving opportunity to young brown and Black kids who may not be totally qualified for the job just yet, but I knew could grow into the job. Just in case anyone thinks this is some sort of preferential treatment or thumb on the scale, let me make just one thing clear: You're damn right it is, because every day of the week in Washington, DC, a young white male is given an opportunity to grow into a job when a person of color is an afterthought.

With this experience and approach, I created a power ranking of every great staffer in America who we needed to go after, which basically excluded any white men, save one or two exceptions. The tired "Bernie Bro" narrative popular in the media and on Twitter might endure, but it just wasn't the reality for us in 2020. My list ended up at 163 people, who I then started calling individually one by one, taking them to coffee or to lunch all through November and a lot of December. Of course, we expected there would be a lot of white men working on the campaign. There were, but we knew that we did not have to be intentional about finding them, because they are so well represented in political work.

The top half of the people on my list all went to work for presidential campaigns — they were the Emmy Ruiz's, Dan Sena's, and Natalie Montelongo's of the world. Some just couldn't commit to a candidate yet. Some of them didn't like Bernie Sanders. Some of them were very interested. I also went back to Bernie 2016 folks to see if I could steal them away from their great jobs. I remember having a great lunch with Farah Melendez, political director with the Democratic Attorneys General, and Dulce Saenz, who has a successful career in real estate and political consulting in Colorado. Even if people couldn't make the move because of recent promotions or they were happy where they were, we wanted to cast a wide net to get top notch Latinas and women of color in the leadership of the campaign, so I began that work early.

But I just knew from learning the lessons in 2015-2016 that we had to do things differently. We also have to keep in mind what we had just witnessed and lived through. I was doing these interviews during a transformational time in American politics. We had not only won back the House of Representatives, but in the process we had elected some amazing young women and women of color, like Alexandria Ocasio-Cortez, who shocked the world when she beat a Democrat in leadership. We will talk more about Ocasio-Cortez's impact on our campaign in 2020 later on.

My long nights consisted of interviews and focused on identifying prospective staffers. We needed to have staff quickly in positions of power, even though we didn't have a way of paying anyone yet, or even know if there would be a campaign. So one of my major jobs for December became to find a campaign manager.

We were looking for somebody very senior that was not a white male. We wanted to get past the false "Bernie Bro" narrative and the accusations that had been made against the campaign in 2016 about sexism. We wanted the culture to be different from the top down, and we had more time to build something this time.

At the beginning of January, I started having one on ones with these people who could be the manager. For many of them, I would do a pre-meeting to see if they should meet with me and Jeff Weaver together.

Once we had interviewed a lot of people, the only moment I'll ever think of myself in the same breath as Dick Cheney arrived. As he had interviewed people to be George W. Bush's vice president before getting offered the job himself, Jeff came to me and said, "Bernie and I think that you could do this job and we want to know if you could be the manager?"

I was shell-shocked a little bit. Maybe more than anyone at the time besides Jeff and the senator, I knew exactly what was being asked and expected of prospective candidates. I'd been busting my butt to get all these interviews done. I had to analyze not only their campaign prowess to learn if they could handle the job, but also examine if they aligned with the values of Bernie Sanders. It was a big, big burden, and my first reaction was, "I don't know, I need to think about this."

I had spent 10 years of my life building out a successful political consulting firm and creating space for brown people to become consultants in Democratic politics. My first thoughts were worries about my staff, worries about if the firm could go on without me, and worries about my family and friends. If I'm honest, I was also worried about people attacking me online just because of my role. All these horrible scenarios went through my head.

There were wonderful scenarios, too. This was a chance for a brown person to be a campaign manager for a presidential campaign, and to do something that had never really been done before outside of Donna Brazile. Julián Castro would eventually select Maya Rupert in January. Kamala Harris would go on to announce her campaign and select Juan Rodriguez. We were making headway, and I would have been a big part of that if I would've taken the job.

I told Jeff I would think about it, and this went on for five to six weeks. I was also worried about my past, and the question of whether I really wanted to relive and relitigate a mistake I made 10 years earlier. On the contrary, would it instead finally put it all behind me, so I would never have to worry about pitching clients ever again?

I was so honored that Bernie Sanders had enough faith in me to consider me for the campaign manager role. It meant so much to me, given where I came from, from a trailer house in East Texas, and all the times people judged me based on how I look or how I speak. It would have been the pinnacle of my career, and legitimized me in a world of white consultants who dominate the industry. I felt I could really do the job because I love people, I love leading people, and I enjoy the details of running campaigns. So I struggled mightily with that decision internally. I was staying up late, not getting sleep, and generally freaking out.

There was one phone call that made all the difference in the world to me. By that point, I was calling some of my closest confidants and friends, about ten people, and asking them what I should do. I was telling them to give me the reasons I should do it and all the reasons I shouldn't do it. One of my best friends is Tim Tagaris, whose firm raised the vast majority of dollars for this campaign. He's a brilliant fundraiser, brilliant strategist, and brilliant human being.

He said, "Chuck, there's one thing you should know. There's a million people on the internet who hate Bernie Sanders with every fiber of their being and once you become the manager, they're going to hate you. They're going to attack you. They're going to attack your family, they're going to attack your business, they're going to attack your past. It will all be scrutinized by these people."

He was right. It was that day that I decided I wasn't going to be the manager, because who needs that? But I did decide I would go to Jeff Weaver and beg him for a senior role in the campaign, to run the parts of the campaign that I had been preparing to dive into headlong, ever since Ann Richards teased me about going to work for her in Austin.

The way I saw it, I ended up choosing the community and the kids who worked for me at Solidarity over a sexy role, but I was still going to fight like hell to elect Bernie. That meant finding the right campaign manager fast. Above all, Jeff said, they offered me the role because they trusted me. That was what it came down to. Finding someone that Senator Sanders would trust.

Faiz Shakir was the political director of the American Civil Liberties Union (ACLU), and he was known in the progressive community. Folks like Ari knew him very well. Jeff and I knew of him, but we had to really get to know him fast for a role like this. He's a Muslim-American guy who went to Harvard, salt of the earth, and the more we spoke with him, he just emerged as the right choice.

When I say he had the right temperament, that might sound like bullshit, but guess who you need to balance a candidate that's super wound up all the time and a bunch of people around him that are similar? You need a calm, soothing voice of reason. On an anger scale of one to ten, I never saw him get above a four or five. You can't tell if he's happy or sad. With the ups and downs of a campaign, he proved to be perfect. He ended up being the first Muslim-American campaign manager, which was amazing. I could also throw a rock and hit his house. He lives a block away from me, so I had unfettered access to my manager.

During the many chats we had, especially early on as we built our organization, I can also say Faiz was just as committed to diverse and inclusive practices as I was — and you can tell how seriously I take it. Him having my back on that foundational piece meant a lot to me.

It's also worth noting that every day I watched all the shit that he had to shovel, and I wouldn't have put up with half of what I saw Faiz deal with. I also ended up having a big role in running the states, and obviously our historic Latino program that we ran. Having the flexibility to actually talk through scenarios, budgets, and problem solving with Jeff Weaver on those fronts ended up being the right situation for me.

At one point of the campaign, during a senior staff meeting, Faiz said he was getting 2000 emails a day and hundreds of text messages an hour. So when I say we hired the right person, I mean it.

One of the keys to our Latino program was not having a Latino department. Some people think, how do you not have a Latino department and dominate the Latino vote? When you start hiring in the beginning, you intentionally build out a campaign that is reflective of the community and has amazing people at every level.

So with Faiz being thrown into the deep end of the pool, and Jeff managing all kinds of stuff, I was the one left in charge of hiring and interviewing everybody and putting the campaign together, along with Arianna and a crew of people like John Robinson, who had been with the Senator and the campaign before. My focus at that time became building out the overall campaign and seeding incredible staffers throughout the organization.

The first thing I did was bring on Luis Alcauter, who is a DREAMer and worked under the deferred action status President Barack Obama began. Over five years, Luis worked his way up at Solidarity from being a junior associate to a partner in the firm. When I decided not to manage the race, I knew I needed to put someone in power who could help implement different parts of not just the Latino plan, but also paid communications.

Luis came over because, as he would say, he "was excited to learn new things," just as he had always been. He came to this country undocumented as a kid when he was 13 and graduated from the University of California, out of Fresno. He's a wonderful, down to earth person. One thing that's important to note is that anybody with any power in life has somebody behind them who actually does all the work. Sometimes what makes me a horrible consultant is that I'm really honest and tell people the truth. So I continually lift up Luis, because I may have come up with a plan, but Luis did all of the work.

Luis put all kinds of things together and was my right hand. Bernie Sanders' campaign was ignited by someone like Luis, who was undocumented, and if it was not for deferred action, which hangs in the balance because Donald Trump is a failure for the Latino community, we would have lost his incredible contribution to the campaign.

Luis has now just gotten married, so he will not have to worry about his DACA status anymore. But for the five years he worked for me, I had to run a consulting firm, and then also worry about the status of my employees. That's real life shit that most consulting firms don't have to fucking deal with, but also speaks to the type of connection we established.

I also moved over Eileen Garcia from our team. I met Eileen when I spoke at New York University, where she was a freshman. I told everybody in that class: if you want to be a summer intern, let me know, because we pay our interns at Solidarity. Within 30 days I had heard from one person in that class, and it was Eileen. So, I hired her on the spot. She was the only one with hustle.

She grew up in front of my eyes, went back to college, came back to Washington and then ended up going to work for Bernie Sanders and ran all of the surrogate communications. She's a bilingual, Venezuelan, bad-ass Latina. Yeah, I want a whole bucket of those hired in this campaign.

Briana Blueitt worked for me. She was the first person we brought in to Bernie, an African-American woman from the great state of Texas. I met her in a training course in New York City, where I was training young women to run for office and doing on-camera training. She ended up working on the press team for the campaign, and also working in the surrogate shop. They were a couple of big hires that I hang my hat on, which were really instrumental in making sure every department had a Latino, or a person of color, or a woman leading them.

I reached out to Belén Sisa, another DREAMer and an activist from Arizona. She's also a mentee of Erika Andiola, who worked for the campaign in 2016 and is an incredibly respected advocate for immigrants and their families. I knew she had good lineage, because she'd worked with Erika, who vouched for her.

I brought her in early because she had been doing communications work for NextGen, and I wanted to immediately have a Spanish-language communications person on day one working with the media. Belén was one of our first hires that we brought in. She ended up doing all of the constituency press because we weren't siloed into just Latino work.

The next hire was not only a big one, but it made Bernie Sanders cry. That's why I had to save it for last.

I felt strongly that the political director needed to be a woman and a woman of color. Again, this was about going beyond ideas of what the campaign had been in 2016. We spoke to great people for the role, and again found someone who meant so much to the campaign. I met Analilia Mejia at a Latino retreat put together by Stephanie Valencia, who herself is a great Latina leader, who put together groups from around the country to start sharing ideas on how we can influence presidential elections.

I loved what Analilia was about the first time I spoke to her. She had a working-class background, was half-Dominican and half-Colombian. She was the Working Families Party state president in New Jersey and had worked for labor with SEIU. You literally couldn't find me a more perfect candidate for political director. Again, this is something that can be repeated in future Democratic campaigns. It's not because I'm special or some genius, far from it. It's because I not only had relationships, but I valued continuing to grow my network and finding the next generation of incredible young leaders of color to take over once I retire.

At the end of January 2019, she took the train down to Union Station in Washington to have lunch with me and Jeff, who of course loved her the first time he talked to her. If you made it through Jeff Weaver and Chuck Rocha, we would set up a one-on-one interview with Bernie Sanders for the big senior jobs.

That meeting stands out to me, because I remember the Senator talking to her and asking her all these questions: about what she had done, where she came from, her stance on different issues, what she wanted to see change in society, what she wanted to do on the campaign, and what her philosophy was on organizing.

But it was the last question that really stuck with me, because he said, "What's the most important reason to get Donald Trump out of office?"

And she said, "My kids. My kids are little mixed-race babies with beautiful fuzzy hair and every day that Donald Trump talks about racism and talks about people of color and attacks our community, I worry about my children. And I worry about the way my children will be judged because they are black children and I worry about the effect it will have on them."

She became emotional about her children, and I remember glancing over at Bernie. For the first time in my life, in person, I saw him get emotionally upset, with tears in his eyes. Then they both got up and gave each other a hug. I turned to Jeff and asked, "Is this something that happens all the time?" And he replied, "No, this is not something that happens." Then Jeff said, "I think she got the job."

Bernie has such a love for his grandchildren, like we all do, and I have for my grandchildren. It's just a special love when you're talking about kids. I believe it actually flipped a switch with Bernie and his increased focus on immigration policy, to travel around the country and meet with DREAMers and young immigrants. He would get visibly, emotionally upset talking to children.

Now that it's clear that diversity mattered not just to the campaign, but to Bernie Sanders himself, I want to add two things about the focus on a woman of color for the political director role and our vetting process.

Too often, we act like hiring is rocket science. It's not. In too many cases, if the people in charge are Ivy League-educated white guys, they will hire who they know or who they're connected to through their network. They will value people that look like them, or give a chance to a young kid that reminds them of themselves when they were young. But I was literally the Mexican Redneck with a criminal record, given a chance and given a senior role.

A priority for me was to hire a whole bunch of really talented brown and Black and gay and Asian folks to work in leadership in every department. It skews more Latino because, guess what? I'm the godfather. I'm the old man who knows everybody. The folks I know in leadership are brown. Most of them are half from California and half from Texas. If you're from somewhere else, you have to pick a side. That's just how we roll in the Latino community. My friends from New York and Miami might disagree, but I digress.

The "Bernie Bro" narrative drove me crazy, because I knew the hearts of Bernie Sanders and Jeff Weaver. They empowered me, and I'm the furthest thing from a "Bernie Bro." So I was very intentional about the way I looked at diversity and inclusion, which is also how we built Latino plans in the states — but we'll get to that later on. I had real authority delegated to me. I knew that from the beginning, before the kickoff, this would really define who we are for the rest of the campaign.

I knew we needed more women in power and more women to be given an opportunity. So by the time we filled out every single department at headquarters, they were all run by a woman. Beyond our Muslim-American campaign manager, we had an African-American deputy campaign manager, a woman communications director, a woman running the organizing department, a woman running the video department, and a woman Political Director. The majority were women of color, which didn't get talked about enough in the press. It drove me crazy, as you might imagine.

I want to close by saying the story of redemption is not just the Chuck Rocha story. I'm glad I get to tell a redemption story about the mistakes I've made, and the opportunities I've been given by lots of good folks. But there were many people who worked on this campaign, and in 2016, who had a criminal history, who had made a mistake, who had been to jail. Faiz and Jeff had the same mentality, maybe more liberal than me, and I'm the one with the criminal record. There were, of course, certain lines around abuse of women and children that we wouldn't allow. If you had a drug conviction, if there was something in your past that was 10 or 15 years ago and you paid your price, we gave you a job and an opportunity. Many of those folks got a chance because in 2016 Jeff Weaver banned the box, and in 2020 Faiz Shakir kept it banned.

Being one of the interviewers, I was able to ask people if they had something in their past they wanted to talk about. I told them to be honest. If they lied to me and I found out later, I wasn't going to hire them. It empowered me to look at somebody and say, "You know, I've got a criminal record and I'm a senior advisor here." I was the perfect person to ask that question.

None of them ever gave us any problem on this campaign. I was happy that Bernie Sanders allowed us to live our values, and give all of those folks a shot to work for us.

Chapter 7

The Heartbeat of the Movement

Who is Bernie Sanders? That sounds silly — because by now we all know who Bernie Sanders is and what makes him tick — but is also critically important when you're running for president again and you want to roll out a campaign with a kick-off that ties back to his roots. When we announced on February 19, 2019, the press wanted to talk about how Bernie was getting more personal, but Bernie hates to talk about Bernie. That's why I love that man. So many campaigns are full of self-serving, ego-tistical candidates.

Bernie doesn't want to talk about himself. He wants to talk about the plight of workers and how everybody is getting fucked. That's what he's talked about his entire career. So getting him to say, "My dad came from another country with no money in his pocket and couldn't speak English," was a big deal. It was something me, Jeff, and Faiz encouraged him to say a lot on the trail.

We wanted to tie him back to his youth in Brooklyn, where we had the 13,000 person-strong kickoff rally on March 2. It was a place we would revisit during the most high-stakes moment in the campaign, which we'll get to in just a bit. After that, we went from there to Chicago, where he spent his college days at the University of Chicago. This is where the famous picture of Bernie getting arrested in the civil rights movement comes from. This was all part of a rollout that Mark Longabaugh had sketched out, before the campaign decided to do its paid media in house.

A lot of times, if you want to get to know a leader, they say look at their company, look at their organization and the values they instill. Don't just talk about it, be about it. One of the things we did that was very important was setting the pay scales so that there was pay equity in every single job. Jeff and Faiz bought into this strongly. Jeff sat at my kitchen table, and we went through what we paid everybody in 2016. In conjunction with suggestions from an outside women-led firm, we made sure we had pay equity across the organization.

Regardless of gender, race, or sexual orientation, you all made the same amount of money for the same position and from one state to another. I was really, really proud of that. Every state director made the same amount of money, every state field director made the same amount of money, and every assistant to a state director made the same amount of money. We had pay equity across every single part of this campaign.

Bernie Sanders also wanted his presidential campaign to negotiate a union contract with its workers, which was historic. You already know my deep love for unions, but this was coming from the top. I had a relationship with lots of different unions. I ended up reaching out to Local UFCW 400, which represented employees at my consulting firm and all across Washington and Maryland. I told them we were going to be doing this. I couldn't organize the union for them because I was management, but I would welcome them in, if they wanted to talk to employees.

Sitting on the management side was really weird, but at least I was joined by a lawyer we hired named Jean-Marc Favreau. He had only negotiated contracts for labor unions, and this was the first time he ever negotiated something from the management side. We would have never gotten through this contract negotiation without him, and I was proud that it resulted in a really fair contract.

People worked a max of 50 hours a week. The contract included mental health benefits. Interns made $15 an hour, and $20 at the DC headquarters because of the cost of living. Living through 30 years of campaigns, I knew what it was like to be an underpaid and overworked staffer. On top of that, everyone had Cadillac healthcare.

Like I said, becoming the first presidential campaign to agree to its workers unionizing was a big deal. I felt like I was coming full circle in a way. As Faiz said to the press at the time, we were proud to uphold Bernie's commitment to collective bargaining rights and a strong labor movement, achieving some of the strongest standards for campaign workers in history and setting the bar higher for the next generation of campaigners.

Briana, who moved over from Solidarity, took the lead in organizing that union. With my union steward background, I was like a proud father as I watched her grow into being a union activist. She'll remember that experience for the rest of her life, and it'll help her through everything she does moving forward.

We built out the headquarters, the different departments, and had all of our state directors for Iowa, New Hampshire, South Carolina, and Nevada in place by March. But this was also the time I was finding my role. It never was about authority with me. I just wanted to help Bernie Sanders win. So there were pieces of the campaign that I locked onto like a pitbull and hung onto, like hiring, until we brought on Rikimah Glymph to do human resources.

Bernie was traveling around the country holding blockbuster rallies, which was the province of Ari and Faiz. Still, somebody had to be in charge of building out the early states, running the campaign day to day, and communicating with voters. Jeff said to the team early on: he and I were going to focus on the states, and Faiz would run the headquarters and the press and the traveling roadshow. The campaign had also decided to bring its paid media in-house. Jeff oversaw that effort, with the help of a talented team of video and digital staff. I also had budget authority, which distinguished Bernie Sanders' campaign from so many others in 2020, and in the history of American politics.

I've worked intimately with all of the Latino nonprofits across the country from the National Council of La Raza (now called UnidosUS), Latino Victory Project, Voto Latino, Mi Familia Vota, and many others. These groups all do critical, amazing work, but they all have one thing in common. They've been woefully underfunded. They never have the resources to do the kinds of programs that would reach as many Latinos as possible.

I used to be one of those donors when I was the political director of the Steelworkers. I sat in those big fancy meetings and worked with folks to determine who should get the money to go do the voter contact. The Latino vote was always an afterthought. There was always something new and shiny like, how do we get suburban women to vote for this Democrat? Now it's, how do we go get these Donald Trump people who voted for Barack Obama in the past? There was always this overarching narrative that I just couldn't stand, that Latinos don't vote.

I can guarantee you one thing: Latinos damn sure ain't gonna vote if we don't spend any money talking to them. Those Latino groups allowed me and my firm to work in communities all across the country — to understand the cultural nuances of a Cuban in Miami, a Puerto Rican in Orlando, a redneck Mexican like me in San Antonio, a Dominican from New York, or an East Los Angeles, La Raza, low rider, go get it son, bad-ass. For my political friends that still don't get it, all of these people show up as Latino on the voter file, but they couldn't be more different.

When establishment consultants do spend any money on Latinos, the low-budget program is usually just Mexican Spanish. Maybe they Google translate some television ads they ran in English, with no message testing in Spanish. Not only is the work done half-ass, it's done half-heartedly. I've watched these Latino groups all beg for money, and never get to actually run the program they want to run. You better believe that when I was given the keys to the car, and the money to actually make it go, I was going to seize that opportunity.

That kind of investment in the campaign was something Bernie Sanders prioritized. But I also found out another key aspect of who he is, when I got a call one day after the campaign kickoff. It said simply, "Bernie wants to see you."

I was like, "Oh shit."

I couldn't figure out why Bernie would want to see me, but this is what makes Bernie so great. We didn't have a lot of consultants besides me, Ben Tulchin, HaystaqDNA, and Tim Tagaris. That's another thing you need to know about Bernie. He doesn't like the whole consultant class very much. But Bernie wanted to have a one-on-one sit down, with only Faiz as a witness, to talk about not making too much money on the campaign. He knew that the money that was raised for his campaign came from hardworking men and women all across the country, $5 and $10 at a time. He found it so powerful, and he disliked consultants so much, that he needed to have conversations with the few that he did have working for him, the ones that were part of the family.

"You can make some money," Bernie said, "but I don't want you building a second home somewhere." His message was that I needed to keep my prices down, because we had a bigger role to play in building the revolution than making money.

"I trust you, Chuck," he continued. "I remember, Chuck, the first time me and you sat down at the Chinese restaurant. I liked you then and I like you now and we're going to do great work. I just needed to have this face to face with you to say, I don't want to see your name in the Wall Street Journal talking about how much money you're making in this campaign."

Bernie didn't like the oppo hit by our opponents that led to an unfair article that had come out about his consultants in 2016. Here he was making sure everyone knew that no one was above the campaign and the people. I told Senator Sanders that he didn't have to worry about me: I was still charging Mexican redneck rates.

Finding my role was a combination of staying away from scheduling, advance work, and rallies, but owning the strategy of how to win the campaign in the states. Beyond keeping my rates down, this included working together with the state directors on budgets and hiring their field directors and other senior staff. The work of diversity and inclusion didn't end at the headquarters. In these critical roles on the ground, we continued to ensure there were Latinos, women, and people of color in positions of power in all of those. As you'll see, this was a big part of winning in Iowa, Nevada, and California.

The very first budget for Latino outreach was put together in April of 2019. It came out of an ad hoc committee of Latino staff from across the campaign, because we didn't have a siloed Latino department. It included constituency organizing manager Basilisa Alonso, who was a driving force in putting the group together, as well as Luis, Analilia, Belén Sisa, Amanda Arias, Eileen Garcia, and Julia Santos.

Julia came from the Senate office's policy department, and joined the campaign policy department. When I was told she wanted to join, but they weren't sure if there was room for her, I said hire her tomorrow. We need more women of color in positions of power. We all sat in my office and detailed on a whiteboard all the different ways we needed to talk to Latinos, beginning with the first four states.

We didn't have to meet again about building the Latino program, because I incorporated all of their input into developing the strategy and the budget for the plan. I was helping elect Bernie Sanders, which meant we put Latinos in a room and gave them voice. The overarching theme that emerged was that Latino outreach should be an integral part of the entire campaign.

We got prices for a major plan to see what they would say no to. Our plan included reaching out on everything from Spanish-language newspapers to digital to mail, with the knowledge that we might not want to go on television too soon and alert other campaigns and the media about what we were up to. Luis did all the work of actually compiling the budget, and it was millions and millions of dollars.

I presented the budget to Jeff Weaver. I told him we needed to start early. I ended up getting 90% of what I asked for. The only thing we ended up cutting, as the campaign progressed, was a small bit of Latino mail in one state.

Once we went beyond the first four states, the budget for the 2020 Bernie Sanders campaign Latino program came out to $15 million, including staff salaries. If you remember in 2016, when I presented everything from the Cadillac package to the Pinto package, Jeff agreed to the smallest one. In 2020, there was no doubt. It was the Cadillac package all the way.

Just because I didn't bring the ad hoc committee together again, doesn't mean they stopped meeting. We got together a month later. They came to me with concerns about immigration policy, and they would prove to play an integral role in crafting the heart of Senator Sanders' immigration policy.

Bernie Sanders had his heart in the right place on immigration during the 2016 and 2020 campaigns, but no one is perfect. The way he talked about immigration sometimes sounded differently to a Latino staffer, especially those who worked in the immigration space on the ground for years before joining the campaign. He was steadfast in his opposition to disgusting Trump policies like putting children in cages and separating them from their families. On everything from migrant caravans to detention centers, staffers wanted to make sure the man they looked up to was defending immigrants at every turn, with the most progressive immigration policy ever created.

They invited me to their next meeting, filled me in, and asked if a group of them could continue to meet, with my blessing, to bring in all the immigrants who worked on our staff at the headquarters (which was about a dozen by that point in May). They included DREAMers, formerly undocumented people, and immigrants from Africa and other countries. Again, we had been intentional in our hiring.

I was proud to see that they would meet on their lunch breaks or after work, because of how seriously they wanted to see changes in this country. Since they all worked in different departments, it was not like they could just disappear for an hour at work. Everybody had a job to do in their own department.

After they started self-organizing, I sent an email. That was probably the first time I cashed in my senior role on the campaign. I told the department heads that their staffers were helping me develop the immigration platform. I asked them to please allow them to meet during business hours, so they wouldn't have to do so on their lunch break, or before or after work.

Empowered to have their regular meetings, they began by

building off of the 2016 policy. They weren't trying to do the job of the policy department, but instead provided a rich level of input from immigrants who had lived experience. As a third-generation Texan, it was the single best learning experience I'd ever had when it comes to policy, because I didn't know all the integral details or the failures of our immigration policy.

I learned things about how a violent criminal is defined, about asylum cases, and how detention centers are run. It was very eye-opening for me. On May 18, I sent an email to my superiors. I told them I'd been meeting with these staffers, and that they needed to meet with them and fill Bernie in.

"With the Telemundo interview coming up in San Francisco and the first debate being held in Miami this issue could not be more timely," I wrote at the time. "They want to bring solutions, not just complain about our messaging. They represent every dept in our campaign, comms, policy, organizing, political and advance."

Jeff, to his credit, immediately said, "Yes, I'll meet with them." A couple days later, he said he had talked to Bernie, who thought it was an awesome idea.

Our immigration plan was ready by the Summer of 2019, and the young folks got about 99% of what they wanted. The big thing was an immediate halt on all deportations. Bernie had already been on record for years calling for an end to private detention facilities. I do give Julián Castro, who released his plan early, credit for elevating the issue nationally in debates. But a little known fact is that Analilia and I were looking for the right moment to unveil this major policy. We thought the UnidosUS conference in San Diego in July, near the border, was the perfect moment. That's when tragedy struck.

I was personally so excited to unveil this policy. We brought along Alex Jacquez, who we hired from the Senate office to work in the policy department. I credit Josh Orton for empowering Alex to do a lot of work on the immigration policy. I was thrilled, because Alex's father Albert Jacquez (who was a mentor of mine) was the legislative director at Unidos and was running the convention. Sadly, a dinner during that trip was the last time

I saw his father, who passed away later that summer. All of that was surreal. But it was during Bernie's flight out to California that everything changed. A white supremacist with hate in his heart drove to a Walmart and started shooting Latinos, just because they were brown in fucking El Paso.

The whole country was reeling from this horrible, tragic event. Latinos and Texans and many around the nation were mourning, so we decided not to release our immigration plan. Bernie wanted to talk about gun violence, about the impact of racism in our country, and about what happens when those two clash, so that's what his speech (written by Jeff and David Sirota) was about that day. Across the country, Latinos felt vulnerable. Being from Texas, and growing up around guns and being a part of the immigrant community, it just really hit home.

You see, if there's anybody who understands racism and hate, it's Bernie Sanders. When he talks about growing up in a Jewish community in Brooklyn, seeing folks with tattoos on their arms with numbers from the Holocaust, that's incredibly powerful. None of us have lived through that. But too many of us, if you're brown or Black and if you were raised in the South and many other places, you know about the stain of racism in this country.

This is who Bernie Sanders is. A man who deeply cares about workers, about inclusion and equality, and about stamping out hate in all its forms. By this time in the campaign, at the end of the summer and heading into the fall, we knew we were doing well with Latinos. The first national Latino poll from Univision in the summer bore that out. The poll showed Biden 20%, Sanders 19%. We were on track. We were tied with the former vice president of the United States.

But there is one more part of this story from 2019 that crystalizes not just who Bernie Sanders really is, but what he means to the movement — to everyone from hard working Latino voters, to its youngest rising star.

By the Fall, a lot was going well, but Elizabeth Warren was the frontrunner. We were bunched at the top of the polls with her and Joe Biden. Then, at the beginning of October, we faced what was the darkest moment for me and the campaign.

It was early in the morning. I was sitting in the locker room of my gym, when Jeff Weaver called me. Now, we're pretty different, but nothing is more different than our sleep schedules. I go to bed by 10 pm every night, and I'm up by 4:30 am every morning. Jeff stays up all night, and sleeps in every morning. It was a lot like working different shifts back in that rubber plant. So I knew something was really wrong.

"Something's happened to Bernie," he said, his voice shaky. "He's had an episode with his heart. We don't know if it's a heart attack. We don't know what it is, but it's not good." Bernie was in Las Vegas, while Jeff was at the headquarters, meeting and holding calls with staff. I'd never heard Jeff sound that way. It scared me.

We talked. We didn't know if we were going to be able to go forward. We didn't want to say anything yet to the staff, but we made some initial inquiries about what it would take to shut the campaign down, if that became necessary. Our first priority was Bernie's health; we could give a shit about the campaign.

This was a man I loved and admired, and Jeff had been around for 35 years. So I just sat down and cried at my locker after I let Jeff go. Faiz was going to be heading to the senator. Jeff needed me back at headquarters. I had to get back to the office.

I think I reached out to Arianna Jones, who is another unsung hero of this campaign. She holds everything together: there is no job too small for her, or too big. I joined her at the office, along with Mike Casca and Sarah Ford, who both led the communications department.

One thing that sticks out in my mind about that time: while many reporters were respectful, some were being very crass, asking if he was alive or if he was dead. I just watched how Arianna and Mike were reacting, and how disgusted they were with how some of the reporters were circling like buzzards around a man that we love and admire, who had just had a health episode. We all went back and looked at the video of the event he was at the night before. We noticed that he had to sit down during his speech. He never does that.

Arianna and I felt like we needed to address the staff. Reports were starting to come out, and there were a couple hundred young staffers who needed an update.

I guess a sense of being the father figure kicked in. I said I would address them. I remember getting on the elevator and trying not to look at Arianna. Every time I looked at one of the staffers, I would start to cry. We pulled that staff meeting together, and everybody's eyes were on me right there. I could tell from the looks on their faces that they were deeply worried.

I told them that we knew he had a health episode, that we thought it was his heart, and that we were waiting for more information. At the very end, l said, "we're going to get through this together," and walked out. I didn't want everybody to see me crying.

I collected myself outside. I realized I couldn't just walk out, so I went back inside to shake everybody's hand, look them in the eye, and tell them it was going to be alright as they walked out of that meeting. It's a day I'll never forget. It was one of the saddest days of my life.

Jeff called me later. He said, "I just talked to the old man."

Now, nobody on this campaign calls Bernie Sanders the old man, except for Jeff Weaver. Jeff was a Marine. It comes from naval tradition that the captain of a ship, even if they are 30 years old, is the "old man" on the ship. There was no doubt that Bernie was the captain, and that Jeff was and is his loyal lieutenant.

Jeff said Bernie was up, and in good spirits, sounding like his regular self. "Turn everything back on," was the directive from Jeff. "He's going to be fine. This won't be a problem." He told me to make sure we get everything back up, if I had put anything on hold in the last 12 hours.

That was followed by a much more concerning call from Jeff. His latest update was from the doctor, who said they still did not have a final sense of what Bernie's recovery would be like.

Jeff was very concerned that Bernie would go out too quickly. "Even if we could put him back out there," Jeff said, "I would never do that because I would never want to hurt him." We put things back on hold, and decided to freeze hiring until we had a better sense of things.

I had all these emotions running through my head. We all loved Bernie, and a movement that we knew was such a noble cause. Against all odds, Jeff Weaver gave me one final call the next morning. He said, "Turn her back on." I replied, "You're killing me here. What do you mean?"

The doctor had returned for the next 12-hour visit. The doctor said that Bernie's heart was close to 100%, and he was going to make a full recovery. Jeff reported that Bernie was up and acting like his old self, after making a dramatic turnaround overnight. He said it looked like he had some blockage in an artery or two, and that they opened those back up. Bernie was going to be better than before. In fact, he was. I remember Jeff signing off on mail later in the campaign. He could instantly recognize whether a picture in the mail was taken before or after Bernie's heart incident by Bernie's skin tone. We made sure only to use pictures taken after.

That was the craziest 48 hours I'd ever spent in a campaign. I almost lost my candidate, who I admired more than anyone. One consequence of this harrowing event was that like a lot of the hardest times in life, you find out who your friends are, and who has your back. Hell, you find out what it means when someone really has your back.

Alexandria Ocasio-Cortez established herself as a star in the progressive movement and the Democratic Party. But what does that mean? It can be hard to know the true measure of a person, when they're such a public figure. Well, she showed her true colors to Bernie Sanders and the whole campaign, when she called him while he was still in the hospital recovering from his procedure.

She told him she was with him and was going to give him her endorsement. She was always going to endorse him, she said, but she was just going to wait till later. But you're going to need it now and we're all going to circle our wagons and you're our leader, she told him.

That right there made me love AOC. It reminded me of friends that had my back during the struggles in my life. In that moment, Bernie Sanders came to learn that AOC and a number of people didn't turn their back on him. Those people put their heads down and made this campaign work.

Ocasio-Cortez's endorsement was part of a shift from a dark and uncertain time for the campaign to a thrilling, block-buster rally in Queens, NY, that changed the tenor of the race. Remember the kickoff rally with 13,000 people? Well, how about 26,000 of our progressive friends coming to watch Bernie — back stronger than ever — coming on stage to AC/DC's Back in Black, clasping the hand of the young Latina leader who is as much of a progressive warrior as he is?

She used the term of endearment for Bernie, Tío, which means uncle in Spanish. It's one so many Latinos adopted for him. In my life, I've had friends who call me Tío, using it for an older male figure who is trustworthy, like family.

"I call him Tío Bernie," AOC said that day. "Maybe to my goddaughter he's abuelo, maybe to some others he's brother, but he's my Tío Bernie Sanders," she told the crowd.

Bernie Sanders had something special up his sleeve, beyond proclaiming "I am back," like he was Michael Jordan coming out of retirement.

"Take a look around you and find someone you don't know — maybe somebody who doesn't look kind of like you. Are you willing to fight for that person as much as you're willing to fight for yourself?" Bernie said, with an awe-inspiring appeal that went viral, reverberating across social media.

"Are you willing to fight for young people drowning in student debt even if you are not?" he implored. "Are you willing to fight to ensure that every American has healthcare as a human right even if you have good healthcare? Are you willing to fight for frightened immigrant neighbors even if you are native-born?"

Bernie Sanders is a dynamic leader of our movement. People think they know who he is, but this is a real portrait of him and what he values. He's not a god, and he's not a mythical figure, but he is a man that we all busted our ass for. As we'll see, he's a leader that so many Latinos and young people and con-stituencies all around the country looked to: somebody who was fighting for all of us.

That's who Tío Bernie is.

PART THREE:

TÍO BERNIE IS BORN

Chapter 8

"Latinos Don't Vote": But They Were the Difference in Iowa

By the time Iowa rolled around, Elizabeth Warren had collapsed since the Fall. At the end of the year, Senator Sanders came back stronger than ever. As the calendar turned to 2020 and the mad dash to the Iowa caucuses, we were in position to do well. It was because of the under the radar work we had done with Latinos.

I have a love-hate relationship with Iowa. During my three decades in politics, I first learned the intricacies of the Hawkeye State in 2004, when I took a leave of absence from the Steelworkers for eight months to move to Iowa. I helped Dick Gephardt run for president as his labor director. In 2008, I worked there with some young guys named David Plouffe, Bill Burton and Travis Lowe, as well.

Learning about Iowa, the texture of the small communities, and how exactly the caucus works was invaluable for me. I learned how things like the math that determines viability to win in the room and caucus-goers' second and third choices can really make a difference. With that being said, the Iowa caucus is the craziest thing that we willingly do every four years. After this cycle, maybe that will change in the future.

To understand where we ended in Iowa — dominating at Spanish-language caucus sites, with Latinos playing a pivotal role in effectively tying Pete Buttigieg in state delegates and winning the popular vote by 6,000 votes — you have to know where we began. Again, a common refrain was true: Jeff Weaver was all in, baby.

In an email to Bernie Sanders 227 days before the Iowa caucus, on June 21, 2019, Jeff Weaver was thinking about Latino voters in Iowa, flagging the possible universe of voters to the senator as he headed to the NALEO conference.

"There are somewhere between 30,000 and 60,000 Latino voters in Iowa," Jeff wrote to the senator. "Only a couple thousand participated in the caucus last time."

Weaver's message was that it could be a big opportunity for us, as popular as Bernie had been with Latinos in the past. A smile broke across my face when I read that email. I knew what Jeff was really doing. He was never going to tell Bernie Sanders exactly how much money we were going to spend in Iowa. It was crazy amounts of money, and we never talked about it with anybody.

Jeff was laying the groundwork and the strategy with the senator, who he knew better than anybody. One way of seeding buy-in early was to show him the potential of the organizing we could do on the ground.

We found a universe of around 50,000 Latinos in Iowa that we were going to talk to. We started talking to them nine months out. Because I was heavily involved in the paid communication, I knew when all the mail was going out, when most of the radio was going to happen, and when the digital was going to happen.

I thought it would be super cool, as both a narrative and as a way of showing how serious we were in speaking to the community early on, to send our first piece of mail in Iowa in Spanish and English, as a bilingual piece of literature. We hadn't sent any mail out in Iowa yet in English. I knew that one way of silencing the narrative that Bernie didn't speak to people of color was to be able to say that the first time we talked to anybody in Iowa, it was in Spanish.

In the end, we sent as many pieces of bilingual mail to voters in Iowa as we did to regular voters in Iowa. That's never happened before. It was all part of the intentional calculation, that if you invest early in this community, it will turn out for you.

Even in a state whose population is 90% white, we built diversity and cultural competency into the team on the ground. It started with our senior advisor out there who had worked on our last campaign, Pete D'Alessandro. No one knows the lay of the land in Iowa better, including every preacher, local union leader, prospective staffer, and all the reporters.

Using his recommendations and relationships, we reached out to Misty Rebik to be Iowa state director. She was an integral part of putting in place the machinery to shock people with our Latino organizing in the state. Cultural competency might be old hat for some, or a new term for others, but Misty basically embodies the concept and why it's so critical. She's a bilingual white woman who has been organizing in the Latino community for years in Iowa. She sure as hell knew more than me about the unique characteristics of the community in Iowa and spoke better Spanish than me, too.

She brought on a young man named Oliver Hidalgo-Wohlleben to do some political work. He ended up becoming the political director of the whole state. His family emigrated from Chile. Together, those two ensured our cultural competency flowed from the top down in the state.

I could imagine some people wondering: in a state that is 90% white, why would you need to worry about 50,000 Latinos? Beyond the fact that this kind of thinking is antiquated in many ways now, I guess in a vacuum, it would only matter if the margin at the end is razor-thin, right? We'll revisit this question later.

I had always argued that the Iowa caucus was restrictive to people participating. It's hard to be available on a Monday night for three hours to go stand in a gymnasium and caucus. What if you have two jobs? What if you have a couple of babies? What if

109

your husband or your wife works at night? What if you're on the swing shift? It's not easy for folks, so the party wanted to have a virtual caucus to make it easier for people to participate.

Needless to say, with what we know of how the caucus turned out, can you imagine tossing some virtual caucus kerosene on top? Anyway, hat tip to our delegate director Matt Berg, who called it early that there was zero chance of this actually happening.

On the other hand, satellite caucuses were created, so you didn't have to go to your particular precinct. These satellite caucuses would be held both in-state and out of state. But one had to apply to create a satellite caucus, so we set out to do so. In our view, it was a way for the Iowa Democratic Party to make the process more open and comfortable for Latinos and Spanish-speakers by adding translators. Giving Matt Berg credit, we took those on. We probably out-organized every other campaign in creating satellite caucuses in-state.

We started concentrating on these satellite caucuses in areas where Latinos live, so we could deem them Spanish-language caucuses with the party and have at least one or two of them in some of the larger counties. Misty's team worked with the organizing team on the ground to start speaking to the community early about the caucus, conducting Spanish-language caucus trainings, hotspot organizing in places Latinos gathered, and making bilingual calls and sending bilingual texts to voters, along with knocking on doors.

On top of all of that, Latinos started receiving bilingual mail from the campaign, getting a piece of mail from Bernie Sanders every other damn week for almost eight months. Then, every time they got in their truck to go to work or to visit family and they turned on their Spanish-language radio station, they heard about Senator Sanders, because we had been advertising on that station for almost five months. If they decided to turn on Pandora or Spotify on their iPhone, we were there too, targeting Latinos for four months.

When retired abuelos or abuelas went to the market and picked up the Spanish-language weekly newspaper that they love

— for reasons that aren't entirely clear to me, but every grandmother does it — we had placed a half-page ad in those newspapers for over four months. In every place where they were working and interacting, you had a paid communication from Bernie Sanders speaking to them.

The paid operation was on top of the organizing I laid out, which included showing up at community events and registering them to vote, in addition to the bilingual caucus trainings. On one of my favorite topics, staffing, we had 27 Latino staffers on the ground by caucus day, with 20 of them being bilingual. Taken together, it was a perfect storm of outreach. It led to Bernie Sanders dominating the Latino vote, which I'll detail at the end of the chapter.

An example of the granular level we were operating on, as we focused on reaching ethnic communities in Iowa, is that on September 2, 2019, Jeff Weaver sent an email to senior Iowa and campaign staff about outreach to various Muslim communities in the state. He talked about identifying local influencers who could work with us on the ground to help get their communities out en masse.

"Those local leaders will then work with our precinct captains to make sure everyone participates and stays through the caucus," Jeff wrote, before talking about doubling down on Latino outreach. He talked about quasi-political organizing events featuring speakers, entertainment and food, but also said he would be very interested "in hearing from folks who have more cultural competency in these communities."

Jeff and I had been working together for a year at this point. I obviously have a lot of love and affection for the guy, but I was really proud to see that my phrases like "cultural competency" — perhaps because I was just that annoying — were now part of his lexicon.

At this point, we had made a real investment in a community that had never been talked to before. Our mail universe was at just under 50,000 people. My friend Joe Henry, who does incredible work for LULAC in Iowa, would argue his organization engaged Latinos seriously in 2016. While he for sure did important work, at this point only 1,800 Latinos had ever been proven to have caucused before on a voter file. There are various issues with matching voters to voter files, but it's just an example of the new ground we were able to break by successfully identifying these voters.

Which is why I was extremely stressed when our diligent pollster Ben Tulchin helpfully noted in an October email that we weren't properly identifying thousands of the Latino voters we were trying to reach. That's a problem, for obvious reasons. At this point in Iowa, as we'll see with Nevada, you get to a point where we've spent so much money on reaching the community — and our polling shows that Latinos are overwhelmingly with us — but we think: will they show up in a big enough number?

If in the past there had been 1,800 Latinos who caucused, we were looking for three or four or five times that number. That kind of number could change the caucus in a multi-candidate race. Our thinking was that just a few hundred votes here or there would make a big difference in the calculation of who actually won the Iowa caucus. Even beyond the math, sometimes the narrative can be equally important.

Ben's analysis was of voters that were ones and twos. When you identify a voter, if they're with Bernie Sanders, they're a one. If they're leaning towards Bernie Sanders, they're a two. If they're undecided, they're a three. A voter leaning towards another candidate is a four, and if they're going to vote another candidate, they're a five.

Misty's team had already identified tens of thousands of Iowans who would caucus and what they would be rated at. That's why field matters so much in Iowa. When you hear people talk about infrastructure in Iowa mattering more than any state, this is why. You have to have an infrastructure, you have to have a personal conversation with so many Iowans, and then you have to tag them in the file as a one through five. That's how you know where you are leading into caucus day. Then you think you have a rough idea about the number you have to reach to win. Even then, there's still viability and second round choices, which only complicates things further. I'm telling you, the Iowa caucus is like a Rubik's cube.

It was very alarming to learn that Ben had matched up the voter IDs with the polling, and found that we had less than 2,000 Latinos identified so far, out of all of the tens of thousands of voters in Iowa. Jeff was just as concerned as I was. He charged me with finding out what was going on on the ground. Misty argued that the IDs were just not showing up in the file the right way, which was probably right. Still, I just knew I needed to identify more voters, bottom line.

I called in my right hand, Luis. I asked him to get me the largest list of phone numbers of registered Latinos in the state. We had 40,000 people, with some 27,000 phone numbers. I hatched a plan to call them with bilingual paid phone callers. Since these are the call centers that I use to do political calls, it's easy for me to do them in 24 hours. We started calling Latinos immediately, to get more IDs to give to Misty and her team on the ground, so they could follow up.

By caucus day, that number had ballooned to over 10,000 Latino IDs that we needed to turn out. It was critical. We had spent over a million dollars on Latino outreach in Iowa that was largely under the radar. It was a large investment, so we needed to make sure that they performed.

I showed up in Iowa two weeks before the caucus. I was finally able to start talking about our work in the Latino community. I had stayed quiet. People who know me can appreciate just what an accomplishment that was. As I've said repeatedly, this was about dispelling the "Bernie Bro" narrative, and showing that our Latino team wasn't siloed off in a corner, a handful of brown people in a back room on laptops.

I had something to prove for everybody, not just for Bernie Sanders' staff, but for every Latino who had ever sat in one of those meetings for years, knowing that people were taking the community for granted or using us as window dressing. Folks didn't realize this, but this was my test market in real-time for Nevada. We had done the same thing in Iowa that we had done in Nevada, but we were doing it on a much larger scale in Nevada. So if my shit went South on caucus day in Iowa, I was going to get on a slow boat to somewhere and never come back.

If we wanted Latinos to show up, we knew we had to have community-based and culturally competent events. Again, I cannot give enough props to Misty and her team, who put together a soccer tournament about ten days before the caucus. It was snowing, and there were two feet of snow on the ground, but they held it at a gymnasium. I'll be damned, but there were eight ethnic soccer teams, five of which were Latino, along with a Bosnian team, as well.

The stands were full of multi-racial, multi-generational, cheering families. It was honestly a beautiful thing to watch. When they got done, we fed everybody and gave them all a bilingual caucus training. That's something that had never been done before, to have a soccer tournament in Des Moines targeting brown folks.

Alicia Menendez, the brilliant MSNBC host, went to Des Moines. She covered what we did with the soccer tournament, before calling me and saying, "Wow, Chuck. That was amazing." She was able to interview people that you would never imagine live in Iowa. In the days leading up to the caucus, we also had the East Los Angeles band Las Cafeteras come out to hold a bunch of mini-concerts in Spanish in the community.

We also got some support from our distributed organizing team at the headquarters, which included Yong Jung Cho and Basilisa Alonso, who worked under Claire Sandberg and Becca Rast, our field and organizing leaders. They realized early on that we could benefit greatly from our national Latino support and energy, by having Latinos across the country communicate with Latinos in key states through our distributed caller and texting program.

That means that if you were a Latino who spoke Spanish and wanted to help Bernie Sanders, we had a special dialer that you could dial into from your home. We would give you a script and train you to talk to Spanish speakers in Iowa. It was incredible. We did the same thing with people that were texting. Let's say you were from New Jersey, and you had a primary that was months away, but you wanted to use your enthusiasm to help Bernie. Well, you could text Latinos in Iowa.

So how did we do? When caucus day arrived, the satellite caucuses came first. At one outside a pork processing plant, there were 24 votes from predominantly immigrant and Muslim-American workers who were taking the time to caucus during their lunch break. We received 20 votes. The other candidates split four.

The regular caucus was at seven, but we continued to receive stupendous reports from the satellite caucuses. There was a community center on the south side of Des Moines where we were getting 80% to 90% of the vote. When all of the satellite caucuses came in, we dominated the Spanish-language satellite caucuses, garnering 95% support. That's not a typo. It wasn't even close. We dominated with everybody who spoke Spanish and caucused early in the satellite caucuses.

At the end of the day, an analysis by the UCLA Latino Policy & Politics Initiative, which also included Matt Barreto, found that Bernie won 52% Latino support in the state's top 32 high-density Latino caucus locations, netting the senator 26 statewide delegate equivalents. Analyzed across all majority-Latino districts, Bernie received support from 65.5% of Latinos, a full two-thirds of them.

Our internal polling from Ben Tulchin showed the same story, with Latino support for Bernie rising 15% in just the three weeks before the caucus, according to an analysis he sent me after the campaign concluded.

In the end, the delegates overall were basically a tie, right? Pete Buttigieg: 564 state delegate equivalents. Bernie Sanders: 562. We had won the popular vote by 6,000 votes. But what does that number look like without an excellent performance from Latinos?

That's why I'm so proud of the work so many of those I've named did on the ground, including Luis and the team at headquarters. Never before in the history of presidential politics did you have somebody running for office where every piece of literature, mail, radio and digital were created by Latinos or Latino-owned firms. You see things like this happen in places like Florida in the last three weeks of an election. You don't see it happen in Iowa or Nevada, and not 10 months in advance.

Ultimately, there was disappointment. Nobody was able to declare victory that night. I felt bad for the talented staff that did such stellar work in Latino precincts, but this next part is for them.

From now on, when anybody runs an election in Iowa, they'll need to have a Latino strategy. It'll be because of a team of bad-ass, young brown kids and culturally competent leaders on the ground. Those leaders showed that if you go and invest in the community early, listen to them and hire them, they'll actually show up and vote for you. You won't hear from a Democratic consultant ever again that it's not feasible to reach Latinos in Iowa. We showed it is.

As we started to flex and show what we had been doing, people started noticing. One national reporter picked up a Spanish-language newspaper, and realized Bernie Sanders was advertising in it. Eventually the reporter confessed something to me. He was having lunch with some of our campaign staff from the headquarters. He talked about how impressed he was with the whole Iowa operation: the TV commercials, the digital, the newspapers, and everything else. That's when somebody from our own campaign spoke up and said, "Well, it doesn't really matter because Latinos don't vote."

After Iowa, he called me to ask me if it felt good to prove that person wrong.

Here's the thing: this was a staffer at the headquarters. Who knows how much experience they had in politics before Bernie 2020? Unfortunately, the thought that Latinos don't vote is something even a lot of experienced political hands think is the case. As I've already explained, there is minimal investment, piss-poor outreach, and half-assed engagement. Then, to top it all off, when races are lost, Latino voters brazenly get blamed for the loss. I mean, it's incredible and sad. To answer the reporter's question, here's what feels good.

After Iowa and after this campaign, that staffer (and so many others) learned one thing beyond a shadow of a doubt:

Latinos do, in fact, vote.

Chapter 9

The Crown Jewel

People think they know Vegas, but it's really just one side of a city I've grown to love. You have the glittering hotels, high rollers, drinks and clubs, and high-priced restaurants and parties. But in those same resorts, you have the immigrant housekeeper cleaning up after your drunk ass, the gaming employee of Mexican descent who's been there for decades, and the majority women, immigrant, Latino — and incredibly influential — Culinary Union.

You have working-class East Las Vegas: it's Cardenas supermarket and their incredible breakfast burritos, but it's also the blue collar workers shuffling in and out, filling their carts to feed their families after their shifts on the strip. More than 80% of all Latinos in Nevada live in Clark County. Beyond the glitz and glam, it's a community of Americans, with kitchen table fears and concerns like anyone else, but characteristics all its own and unique passion points like immigration.

For candidates jockeying for position after predominantly-white Iowa and New Hampshire, it's notably the first early state on the nominating calendar with a diverse population available. It was also where the Bernie Sanders campaign was making a defiant stand, a major step in showing that the senator's coalition was a multiracial, multigenerational one. A place to put the "Bernie Bro" narrative I've mentioned to bed for good. All because we had started the Latino program nine — yes, nine — months earlier. All for this very moment.

After we kicked off the campaign in the Spring of 2019, Bernie Sanders had been invited to come to Las Vegas to speak to the Machinists Union, which is run by one of my dearest and oldest friends, Bob Martinez. Bob is from Dallas/Fort Worth. He started as a union steward, then a chief steward, before working his way up to be the international president of the Machinists Union. Given my background, I could not be more proud to see a Latino running a major national labor union.

As I've said, I rarely spend much time out on the road with Bernie. I was way too busy helping to run the states and the Latino program. But when something is important to the Senator and important to a connection I had, I was really glad to do it. I went out to Las Vegas early to meet with Bob and his team, who told me that it would be a really friendly crowd and how much his membership loves Bernie. We spent the day together. Bob told me how proud he was of me. We had lots of mutual respect for how far both of these old Mexican redneck farm boys from East Texas had come. The next day, Bernie flew into town.

In the green room, Bernie met the union leadership and took lots of pictures. On stage, he killed his remarks as usual. I mean, Bernie got like six standing ovations. It was a great day. We get in the van. The senator wants to eat before our flight. But he doesn't want airport food. "I bet they have some good restaurants here in Las Vegas," he says. That was music to our ears. But just about the time my gears started moving on where we could eat, Bernie said, "I bet there's a Waffle House or a Ruby Tuesdays."

We ended up at a Waffle House. By now, it's clear that what you see is what you get with Bernie. Of course, it was like a rock star walked in. Bernie got eggs, bacon and toast. It's not complicated with Bernie Sanders. As he loves to do, he went to the back to meet the folks working in the kitchen. He asked them if they were going to caucus for him.

The caucus was almost a year away. It's relatively new

to Nevada anyway, so people said, "Yes, we're going to vote for you!"

"No, I need you to caucus," he responded. "Yeah, we're going to," they said. "We love you, Bernie!"

That moment left him with an impression that few in the state, especially these Latinos working in the kitchen who he would need a year later, even knew what a caucus is. So as he had done the year before, Bernie wanted details from me on what we were going to do to get Latinos to vote.

I told Bernie we were going to go into the community, listen to them, educate them about the caucus, and ask them for their support. He told me we needed a plan. It's very intimidating for people to caucus when English may not be their first language.

"I need you to put together a real plan, Chuck. This is what this campaign is about. We need to get new people to come vote and it's your job."

That was it. Bernie, in his voice, telling me it was my job to get Latinos out, not just in Nevada, but everywhere for this campaign. "All of those people back there in that kitchen, they'll vote for me, but they're not going to caucus. You have to figure out how we go get them to caucus."

That incredible exchange with a great (but no nonsense) man, is a window into the stress I was feeling to deliver in Nevada, which I briefly touched on earlier. At the end of that car ride with Bernie, I told him we were going to open an office in the community to start talking to them early, where we can invite them to do caucus trainings in Spanish and hand them bilingual literature — not just for them, but for their families, as well.

That's exactly what we did. It was the bedrock of our work on the ground and the fruits it would bear. The seed was planted in a van leaving a Waffle House with Bernie Sanders a year earlier.

The day after the New Hampshire primary, I got on an

airplane in Washington and headed to Nevada. We had basically tied Pete Buttigieg in Iowa and edged him in New Hampshire, but beyond what it could tell us about the makeup of our supporters, Nevada could represent real momentum.

There were certain things in my mind that I knew beyond a shadow of a doubt. I knew that we'd spent a whole lot of money talking to Latinos who had never been talked to before. We had started earlier than anybody ever had. We'd run the most culturally competent paid communication program that had ever been run in the history of presidential politics, but none of that guaranteed that Latinos would actually show up.

When it came to the caucus, they wanted to increase participation, and for it to be more inclusive. So they built in four days of early vote. I needed to get my ass on the ground to make sure that we were going to maximize Latino early turnout.

The Culinary Union had issues with Medicare for All, so the most powerful union in the state basically issued an anti-endorsement of Bernie Sanders. They ran a campaign with their stewards to get their members to vote for Joe Biden, and I would eventually see the leaflets to prove it. The leadership was so solidly behind Joe Biden that if he had come near the top in Iowa and New Hampshire, my sources tell me the Culinary Union was ready to endorse Joe Biden. They had already printed up the bumper stickers.

Later, I'll explain how our campaign got around leadership and spoke to the members. By now, things were serious, and this is an example of that. Our campaign had become a threat. Establishment opposition to Bernie also ramped up in Nevada, with one Israel-focused group running ads against us. Another pro-business group, affiliated with Senator Joe Manchin, started doing so, as well.

As I promised Bernie, we opened the East Las Vegas office in June of 2019, in the heart of the Latino community. I wanted them to know that we were coming to their community, and that we respected them. The next thing we did was hire a state director, Sarah Michelsen, from the neighboring state of Arizona, who had been embedded and working deeply in the Latino community in Arizona and ran the entire progressive table.

That means she brought all the organizations in Arizona — the unions, the progressive groups, the women's groups, the environmental groups — together to run campaigns in Arizona and helped elect Krysten Sinema as senator in 2018. Peter Koltak joined her as a senior advisor. Our very next hire, Susana Cervantes, was the statewide field director. I went and recruited her myself to have this job, because it was going to be so critical to have her on the ground. She grew to be one of 76 Latinos working in the state of Nevada. We had more Latinos working in Nevada than most of the other campaigns had in total staff.

As I've said on television and elsewhere many times, in 2015 and 2016 we were building the airplane while we were trying to fly it. But one thing we knew is that Latinos liked Bernie Sanders. We wanted to see how much they liked him, and how big the universe could be.

In campaigns, you have to identify voters, put them in a spreadsheet, and then cross-match them to a voter file. There were about 18,000 Latinos in Nevada who caucused in 2016, so you start with them. I figured ahead of time that those would be the only Latinos that any other campaign would try to reach, if they spent even $1 on Latinos. My secondary targeting was Latinos who actually vote in congressional races and other primaries, but haven't caucused. There was some overlap, but it added another 20,000 voters. Now, we're at close to 40,000. Almost a hundred thousand Latinos showed up to vote in the last general election. Removing the overlapping voters, we had about another 50,000 voters to add. Now we're in the 80,000 to 90,000 range. My real excitement centered around another 100,000 Latinos who registered to vote since Donald Trump has been president.

So o stress this point, more Latinos had registered to vote in the last three years than had actually caucused in the 2016 caucus. That gave me another expansion of Latinos I figured no other campaign would talk to. You know why? Because these newly registered Latinos have no voting history. Most consultants are not going to waste a dollar talking to a voter who won't reliably show up to vote. If they're not voting, the thinking goes, you would never get them to take the time and show up to caucus.

I knew we had free reign to talk to a group of Latinos for a long period of time that nobody else would talk to.

In the end, the universe of Latino voters in Nevada was 120,000, after beginning with only the 18,000 that had caucused. The idea was to get enough resources to talk to them and motivate them to come out en masse. Like I talked about earlier, I used the same model that we used in Iowa. We had to scale it up greatly and have a much bigger audience.

The second piece of the puzzle was knowing how Latinos felt in the Summer of 2019. We needed to have a baseline of support to know whether our efforts were working. It was almost like the Latino voters in the state were a blank canvas. I wanted to record where they were at, before we started throwing all this paint in the form of mail, newspapers, and television.

I told Jeff I wanted to do a poll in Nevada to get a baseline for the Latino vote. He of course rightfully noted that it was too early. Bernie was never going to approve a poll of Nevada before one was taken in Iowa. As we've stated, the great Bernie Sanders is not a big fan of polls or consultants whatsoever.

I told Jeff I could do the famous Mexican redneck poll with my call centers. It was a problem-solving exercise that goes back to my granddaddy: here's how you get around power structures to get what you want done. I knew we had the phone budget, because I wrote it. I told Jeff, "I'm going to spend a couple thousand dollars and I'm going to call a whole bunch of Latinos in Nevada and I'm going to ask them if they like Bernie Sanders and, if not, who do they like?"

We did a rough phone survey. Our base support in early July was around 32%, with Biden right there with us at 29%, and a couple others near double digits. While I had them on the phone, I also asked them what their number one issue was, so we could fine tune the direct mail and literature we were going to send out. Their answer was healthcare.

You see, Latinos over-index among the uninsured and underinsured. They're younger, there is less fluency, they have less wealth and where there's a high-rate of mixed status families in states like Nevada, there is less employer-based healthcare. So Medicare for All worked, not only because it is the fairest option, but also because many of them understood government-run healthcare through the Medicare taxes they pay or from the countries they came from. They understood that because they had a grandmother or great-grandmother who were on Medicare.

While that was an issue that we used a lot, it just wasn't the first thing I said to a Latino. I wanted to build that relationship first, which was sort of humorous when I brought this plan to Jeff.

"You just told me that the number one issue is healthcare and you're going to lead with immigration. Can you tell me why?" Jeff asked.

I told him we had plenty of time to talk about healthcare, but we only have one opportunity to make a first impression with voters who don't know who Bernie Sanders is. I'm going to open with an emotional issue because it's Nevada, because it's an immigrant community. I reminded Jeff of the speeches he had written for Bernie in 2016, talking about Bernie's immigrant roots. By now, it's clear that Jeff empowered me in a historic way, to his credit and that of the senator. It showed in a moment like this. Jeff didn't question me; he trusted me.

That decision meant Latinos in Nevada and other states were introduced to Bernie through his immigration story. His father immigrated here, he had no money, he had working-class values and couldn't speak English. I didn't really have data backing this up, but I had my gut and my 30 years of experience telling me it was the right approach. If I'm a Latino casino worker in Nevada and the first mail piece I get is, "Hey, I'm this 78-year-old white guy from Vermont, Feel the Bern, come get your free healthcare," I think I'd be a little skeptical. Like, "Who is this guy and how the hell is he going to get me free healthcare?"

The immigration story, rooted in where Bernie and his family came from, allowed young and old Latinos in Nevada to say, "that's just like my dad or like my abuelo or like me." So Medicare for All was a critical issue that we used a lot, but we just didn't lead with it.

X

Shortly after the survey, we created a bilingual literature piece around immigration, healthcare, and jobs, so our volunteers in the state would have something to walk with for door to door campaigning, which we did for a total of nine months. Once we got that up and running, we started a robust and very aggressive mail program.

I'm a mail consultant by trade. With Luis as my right hand, we had a tailored program made by Latinos in house. We sent 16 pieces of mail to Latinos in Nevada. By the time caucus day arrived, that large universe of 120,000 Latinos had received mail from Bernie every other week for eight months.

Beyond the tactics — which were pretty smart if I do say so myself — we had a secret weapon in Nevada, a longtime business associate of mine named Sean Sinclair, who was our production director. We worked together in our twenties, along with a lot of other operatives I've mentioned like Dan Sena and Bubba Nunnery. Sean also helped when my firm was starting up to scale up for big projects I was taking on.

He ran Harry Reid's reelect, who himself is a Nevada institution, and brought us Peter Koltak, so he really knows Nevada. Sean was indispensable. We did all the mail, all the radio, and most everything else in Nevada, not just the Latino program. One thing he did orchestrate, however, was creating a direct mail model for the Latino outreach to make sure we were executing efficiently and not wasting any money. We may not have been the choice of the machine in Nevada, but we beat it in part because of people like Sean.

We sent a bunch of mail. There are consultants who say mail does not move people to support you unless you do a lot of it. I would argue that you don't have to do as much mail as they suggest. I think you just have to make good mail, created with cultural competency at its heart. Our Latino numbers did move, which we'll get to. Ultimately, we spent $300,000 on Spanish-language television as the caucus neared, but $1.2 million just on mail to Latinos in Nevada.

One of the anchors of the mail program was that Bernie

Sanders does so well with Latinos and he does so well with young people. Why not combine the two?

We wanted to figure out the audience that was the young-est and the most Latino that nobody was talking to. I didn't even have to go far for inspiration, because Jeff did this first in Iowa in 2016. So I went back and found a commercial vendor who could go into the state of Nevada and find me a list of 17-year-olds who were in high school and still lived at home. This is how it works.

If you're going to turn 18 before the November general election, you can caucus in Nevada. When the list came back, it ended up being about 40,000 teenagers who would be 18 by the general election, who we could talk to. Now, what you can't do is address the piece of mail to that person because they're a minor, but we could address it to their parents if they were a Democrat or independent.

In really large letters, it was clear that it was really meant for the 17-year-old. We told them, "Let your voice be heard. You can caucus for Bernie Sanders." We did two different rounds of mail to that 40,000-person universe. We actually called their parents to remind them that their kids could caucus, because we knew their parents were Democrats. That's an example of some-thing nobody did in this campaign. It goes against the narrative that young people don't show up. We were going to talk to young people, and they were going to show up.

Mail was the backbone of the program, but it's important to understand the different ways Latinos consume information. For example, my looks may not betray it, but I've got a son who's 30, while I am in my early 50s. When I come home from work, I sit on the couch, going back and forth between a baseball game and MSNBC, while scrolling through my Facebook and Instagram feed at the same time.

My son doesn't own a TV, and he's not on Facebook. Don't you know that it's not really cool anymore? He consumes infor-mation in a whole different way than his father does. Yet on the voter file, we're both Charles Rocha. We were reaching people in their teens and 20s, people in the Charles junior generation. We were also reaching people in the Charles senior categories, and the 60 and 70-year-old Latinas and that generation.

This is where multilayered communication comes in: a fancy way to say talk to them where they are at. So for the Charles juniors, we did Instagram. We did hundreds of thousands of dollars of digital advertising on Hulu and YouTube. We did other platforms where young Latinos were consuming information about Bernie Sanders. Then, even though they were getting our mail, we ran a lot of Facebook ads to middle-aged brown folks in Nevada, as well as Pandora ads. 80% of Latinos over 30 who listen to streaming music do so on Pandora.

Now, if you're reading this, and saying I'm not hip because Spotify is where all the action is at — well, I would only agree with you on the first part. Most young Latinos are on Spotify, but 90% of them are under 18. I am looking for folks who can vote. On Pandora, you get bang for your buck. Not only do I serve you an audio ad, but it includes a banner you can click on, bringing you to the Nevada website to get early voting and caucusing information.

Latinos my age and older like terrestrial radio. We bought a lot of that along with Spanish TV, but terrestrial radio was the most targeted operation we ran. This was how we dealt with the expected outcome that Culinary Union leadership would either endorse an opponent, or actively work against Bernie.

If you've ever stayed in a hotel, and got up early in the morning like me to go to the gym to try to stay youthful, sometimes the housekeeper is already in your room. When this has happened, what do you hear when you walk into that room? Most of the time you have a Latina who's cleaning your room, especially if you're in Las Vegas. Normally she's got your bed sheets ripped back, but she has taken your bedside radio and flipped that thing on to good Spanish music.

She's doing a hard job all day long to take care of her family. There's one thing that always brings her happiness: listening to music that reminds her of home, reminds her of her mother and father, reminds her of dancing with her husband at her kid's wedding. It's music in our community that connects us all. Most of the time housekeepers will turn that on immediately when they walk into a room, and they're listening to that radio. Because I knew these things, I started advertising on La Buena KWIDISF, the radio station in Las Vegas that all of those house-keepers listened to — not one or two weeks ahead of the primary, but six months before the caucus.

On everything from his immigrant family, to his fight to get everyone healthcare, to raising the minimum wage and the importance of criminal justice reform, for six months we had an attentive audience of Culinary Union members. From the radio at work, to the mail at home every other week, to scrolling on Facebook, they were getting Bernie Sanders ads everywhere.

I estimate that every Latino Culinary Union member who participated in the caucus heard from the campaign at least 22 times before caucus day. That's why you saw us not only win the Culinary vote, but also be able to push back against their leadership when they came out against Bernie and actively campaigned in the caucus rooms against Bernie.

As I've shown, I'm not beyond going with my gut when it's informed by things I've learned from Latinos throughout the years, including my own family and friends. The last piece of paid communication involved Spanish-language newspapers, the weekly or biweekly ones seemingly every grandmother or abuelo loves to get. Nobody spends any money in Spanish newspapers. Nobody but me. I didn't want to leave a stone unturned in Nevada. We had a half-page ad in every Spanish-language newspaper that was printed every week for six months.

This goes at an important misconception about Bernie Sanders and his Latino support. When many think about a state like California and about Bernie's national support, they use it as shorthand for young Latinos. But the Spanish-language newspapers are just one example of us talking to Latinos at every single level, including older Latinos. The numbers we'll get to shortly show this: we got all of the Latino vote in Nevada, because we talked to all of them.

You can show up at the last minute, like Mike Bloomberg, and spend a bazillion dollars in the last couple of weeks. It's still not enough to build that relationship. I built trust to get to the point of, why not vote for Bernie? He seems pretty cool. And you know what? I think it'd be nice if my kid didn't have to pay back their student loans.

It also wasn't a big cost endeavor. We put an ad in every single Spanish-language newspaper in the state of Nevada for six months. We spent less than $10,000.

It's important to show this work, and the detail and richness of the Latino program. By November 1, just 15 weeks before the caucus, we must have been in cruise control in the state, right? Wrong.

On November 1, the senior staff received an internal poll from our pollster showing concerning news. Biden was still leading in the state with 25% support, compared to 20% for Bernie. We were leading 28% to 26% with Latinos, but things still were not where they needed to be.

But things continued to improve. The new year brought enthusiasm and new mediums to reach voters as the sprint to the caucus was on.

With the program running on all cylinders, reaching Latinos comprehensively across the state, it was time to unveil our TV ad buy. Most reporters and the other campaigns would only gauge Latino outreach the moment somebody bought a commercial on Univision or Telemundo, so a lot of our program went under the radar.

Six weeks out, people thought Bernie was beginning to target Latinos, because he started TV commercials before everyone else except Tom Steyer. We took the same Bernie Sanders immigration digital ad that had been running for nine months. We made it part of our closing TV push, since everyone was already familiar with that imagery and story. It's like, "Tío Bernie, his daddy didn't have any money when he came here. He's one of us." That ran for three weeks. For the last three weeks before the caucus, we ran something special that we had created as the Iowa closing ad, as well.

We took all of the DREAMers on our staff at headquarters

and formerly undocumented staffers — 16 altogether. I sat down with them and Luis. I told them I wanted the closing ad to show voters that this campaign lives its values, and that we had empowered each one of them to work on the campaign and to run different departments, none of which were a Latino department.

I told them to write a script that would move our people, and say, "Now you've got to show up to caucus." I gave the power directly to them. Neidi Dominguez, an immigration activist who we lured away from the painters union (and just generally a badass Latina), took the lead with Luis. They put the whole thing together.

The closing shot had the staffers in the park in front of the White House. It was called "Nuestro Futuro, Nuestra Lucha" — Our Future, Our Fight. Neidi looks into the camera, and says in Spanish, "Mi gente, it's our moment, we're going to vote for Bernie Sanders." Basically, it's time to show up. The ad included Latino workers, but also our immigrant staff.

The way I knew it worked: when I was freaking out and heading to Nevada, I went to the leadership of the campaign. I said I needed all of the Latino staff, everyone that can speak Spanish, to head to Nevada to help get out the caucus. I'm worried to death. We sent Neidi too, who was the deputy state director. She later told a story of talking to folks while they were waiting in line outside the famed Cardenas supermarket. A woman was pointing at Neidi and talking to her daughter, so she walked over and asked if there was something she could help with? "You're the girl from the TV," the woman said in Spanish, beaming.

I was like, "Oh my God, it worked." It was one of the proudest moments of the Nevada operation.

A few days before the caucus, I had dinner with Congressman Filemon Vela and Cristóbal Alex. One of them was an early endorser of Joe Biden, and the other was the most senior Latino staffer for Biden. Both of them are my dear friends, who I've worked with for many years. We got sushi. They were showering me with comments about how well we were going to do on caucus day.

Of course, that made me even more nervous. Now every-body thinks we are going to win, but we have no way to know who in the hell is going to show up and fucking caucus. I had gone for a relaxing dinner, but it had just made me more uptight.

One reason I felt that way was because there was a prob-lem with the early vote. The party had created strip caucuses, so folks who worked in the Las Vegas casinos had a place to go caucus if they had to work. The next thing they did is create an early vote where people could vote at any early site, and cast your ballot in preference order. They did this on Saturday, Sunday, Monday, and Tuesday before the caucus, to leave a few days to tabulate all of the results. That way, they would have those ready to add to the caucus day total on Saturday. The party promised us that by noon on the next day, they would give us a list of the people who caucused on the first day, so we can stop calling them or reminding them to caucus.

Of course, after day one at noon, there was no data. There was still nothing by 3 pm. No early vote data came at all, until late in the evening on day two. Mind you, this was after the disaster that was the Iowa caucus. Absolutely no one was feeling good at this point.

The problem for Chuck Rocha and my ulcer at the time was that the partial data we did receive skewed dramatically to-wards old white people.

"The modeled support is encouraging but it is still WAY too OLD and WHITE for comfort," our intrepid pollster Ben Tulchin wrote, just days before the all-important caucus. "We will see what today brought us with campus early vote sites, but we will still need a really good turnout with young people and younger Latinos this Saturday to ensure we win by a decent margin."

The majority of people who had voted on day one, from the partial data we received, showed that the majority was older and white. Well guess who doesn't really care for Bernie Sanders? Old white people. It also may as well have been one last blaring alarm that read: "Chuck Rocha, where are the Latinos again?"

We had already added $200,000 to the budget, and rented

132

the awesome neon light trucks. At this point, I was just a mess of calling and texting every Latino, every day, all day long, nonstop. By caucus day on Saturday, I was a bundle of nerves.

One of the things that helped during this time was my beautiful, amazing, intelligent, salt of the earth girlfriend, Ebony. She flew to Nevada so we could be together for Valentine's Day. It's really hard on a relationship when you're working in a campaign. It's doubly hard when you're working on a presidential campaign. We went to dinner, we went to a show, and we hiked the canyon the next morning, before I had to do a bunch of work in the afternoon. Then she got on an airplane, and flew back to Washington. My mother is white, and my father was Mexican. Her mother is white, and her father was African-American and a DC resident. She didn't just accept Bernie immediately — he had to work for her vote, but he got it eventually.

With the stress I was under, she was a real rock for me to hang onto. In the evenings, we would have our phone call, and that would ground me. She told me everything would be alright, no matter what happened. I would be remiss if I didn't mention how critical her support was for me. Thank you.

I started caucus day early in the morning. First, I went to the gym, like most every morning for the last 30 years. I talked to Luis at 6:00 AM. He and a crew of Latinos from headquarters were out putting leaflets and door hangers on people's doors before the sun came up in Latino neighborhoods, to remind them that it was caucus day once they woke up. I want to say that's the kind of soldier you want during a campaign. That's not what he is. Luis was just my incredibly hardworking right hand guy who did all the nuts and bolts of the Latino program. That's who you want by your side when things get tough.

There was nothing else I could do at that point, so Eileen Garcia booked me on MSNBC for a one-on-one interview with Alicia Menendez. Alicia has been a friend for many years, and I was super proud to see a Latina get a show on cable. I then did a CBS interview, and headed to the war room at headquarters.

We had all the TVs on. There were reporters at all the different caucus sites, which was awesome and fascinating and scary as hell, if you were the Mexican in charge of the Latino out-reach for the campaign that needed you to win Nevada.

CNN said they had exit polls by demographic. Here we go! The first exit polls showed Bernie Sanders had 55% of the Latinos that caucused, and Joe Biden had 18%. I was like, sweet baby Jesus, please, please tell me our voters showed up like that. Then, we started winning areas we weren't expecting to win, and it wasn't just Latinos, obviously.

Neidi was a longtime organizer, who worked on the caucuses on the Las Vegas strip, where the door stays open for an hour before they shut it and start counting everybody. In this particular caucus, it was contentious: the room was dead-locked.

All of a sudden, people in the room heard chanting coming down the hall, just three minutes before the door had to close. Suddenly, all of these Somali taxi drivers walked in solidarity together, carrying Bernie signs and chanting for Bernie. They were led by Mexican-American Neidi Dominguez, who organized them around the issue of immigration. We overwhelmingly won that caucus, because she showed up with a surprise attack from the Somali taxi cab drivers. I mean, that's the good shit. That's how you do organizing. It was also proof of something else we saw throughout the campaign. Bernie was popular with Latinos for sure. But he was popular with immigrant communities from around the world — from Africa, from the Middle East, from Asia and every other place.

We had gotten our butt kicked in the strip caucuses in 2016. Not this time. That's when I figured we were actually going to win. We won five of those caucuses, we tied in one, and then we barely lost the last one by two delegates. I thought I was going to cry in front of every person in that room.

Some of the funniest pictures from the strip caucuses were all these Culinary members on the right with Biden signs. They were literally all the union stewards. Then you had all the rank and file members on the other side, holding Bernie signs. They're all hollering at each other, waving their signs.

That was one of the proudest moments of my life, getting

to watch that, knowing I had a big impact on it actually happening. With my union roots, there was not much more gratitude than what I was feeling that day. We had just out-organized the most powerful union in Las Vegas.

The caucus started at noon. By four o'clock, we knew we were going to win, and we knew we were going to win big. Stories from that day are etched into my mind. A reporter called me while I was in the war room and said, "I've been to three caucuses on the east side and there hasn't been another candidate besides Sanders who's even got a delegate yet, you are getting every delegate in every single precinct on the east side of Las Vegas."

UCLA's Latino Policy & Politics Initiative did a precinct by precinct analysis. It found that Bernie received over 70% of the Latino vote in Nevada. Our own polling showed the upwards journey of support from the community. Ben Tulchin found that Latino support for Bernie in Nevada went up 22% in the four months before the caucus.

Let me remind all of you that in the densest Latino neighborhoods, we were blowing it out. There wasn't even another viable candidate. I was like, yes, send me all the reports. By the end of the night, there's a reason why Nevada was the crown jewel: we had done everything we knew to do, in all the right ways. I thought it would be groundbreaking. It ended up bigger than I even expected.

Getting this data, I felt like I was living in a dream. I became emotional when Ben Ray Luján called me. We did such great work together in 2018, because he gave a Latino a chance to be a consultant for the DCCC, and he's been a big supporter and friend.

"Chuck, you don't realize what you've done, but everybody is watching you," he said. "Now everybody knows that if you invest in and respect the Latino community we will turn out. You've changed the game forever for people like me and others who've talked about this for generations." I blubbered my way through the rest of the call, thanked him, and called Ebony.

I told her Ben Ray called to say he was proud of me. As

somebody who grew up without a father around, I always looked for somebody to validate me. I felt like I needed to perform for somebody to say that they were proud of me. It's been hard for me to accept a lot of times, but it's something that I've yearned for and worked towards. As I've gotten older, I've done enough self-reflection where I know I don't always need that. Still, it felt good this time.

Ebony and I had an emotional conversation, as well. Then I went to an after party for supporters, at this little joint somewhere in Vegas with Jeff and the team. People wanted to take pictures with me and shake my hand. It was surreal. I'll never forget this campaign. More than anything, I'll never forget what it meant to win in Nevada, our crown jewel.

Chapter 10

The Behemoth

Coming off the magic of Nevada, we received some props among commentators and the political press. We were emerging as the frontrunners, but we also knew California on Super Tuesday was the behemoth. Political scientists and experts in the state agree on one thing: California is about five or six states combined into one — not just in terms of sheer size, but also in the ways in which the valley differs from Los Angeles, the Bay Area from the Central Coast, and on and on.

When I think about everything that went into winning a state like that, again showing the thunderous appeal of the movement, I'm reminded that it was only possible because of how early we began thinking about the state. How early? Try 2018.

I had a once in a lifetime trip planned for my 50th birthday on December 14, 2018, because I knew the demands the campaign would make on all of us if Bernie decided to run.

I took five of my buddies, and we went to Cuba to go fishing. Anybody who's known me for more than 30 minutes knows that I'm an avid fisherman. I spend a lot of my time advocating for the conservation of the Florida Everglades. It just so happened that most of the campaign ideas that I've had for Bernie Sanders and for Solidarity Strategies came on the front of captain Steve Friedman's fishing boat.

There's very few places in the world that I can go where people aren't tugging at me, my phone's not going off, and I don't feel a constant noise or echo in my head. Being on the front of a fishing boat, it means there's no one within miles and miles of me. It's just me and Steve out there fishing, looking across the sparkling water for a tail to pop up.

On the way, I was super nervous. I was still doing staffing interviews, and quite aware I was going to be literally off the grid for five or six days with no cell coverage. I was standing at my connecting gate in Miami, connecting to my Cuba flight, with these thoughts swirling. That's when Jeff Weaver called, and got to the point.

"Do you have somebody in the Julián Castro campaign?" he asked.

In another hat tip to Jeff's thinking ahead, we had been monitoring the no party preference (NPP) (that's what they call independents in California) rule in California proposed by secretary of state Alex Padilla. It would allow the state government to send all the NPP voters a presidential ballot. As it stood, with two years before the election, they would get congressional, state representative, and city council primary ballots — but no presidential ballot, because it's the only partisan primary. Unlike in most states, California's primaries are nonpartisan. It's what they call a jungle primary, where all the candidates from all the parties are on one ballot. The top two contenders for every race go to the general election, whether they're a Democrat or a Republican. But in California, where much of the voting is done by mail, NPP voters (independents) would not automatically get a Democratic Presidential Primary ballot. Instead, they would need to go through an additional step: either changing their party registration, or specifically requesting a Democratic ballot.

Weaver called me 15 months before the March 2020 primary, while I had visions of casting out my fishing rod on a sunsplashed boat, to see if he could get in touch with Castro because he realized this was going to disenfranchise hundreds of thousands, if not millions, of young Latino voters in California. Jeff planned to ask the Castro campaign to join us in pushing back, to see if we could get ballots mailed out without them having to go through a two-step process.

The reason why young people (and young Latinos specifically) are effectively silenced by the way the California Democratic Party handled NPP voters, is that many young people are automatically registered to vote when they get a driver's license. If the person doesn't pick a political party on the form, they are defaulted to NPP status. As we are increasingly aware of systemic hurdles that have disparate racial impacts, it's time for the California Democratic Party to re-examine the way they treat NPP voters.

We are all appalled when Republicans make people jump through extra hoops to vote. We know that even adding a relatively small obstacle will keep some voters from participating. Of course, those voters are almost always poor or people of color. The California Democratic Party should be doing everything possible to engage young voters and, particularly, young voters of color — not creating hurdles that effectively disenfranchise them. In others words, in the incredibly important state of California, the California Democratic Party should not be silencing the voices of young Latinos in the super important process of choosing the Democratic Presidential nominee.

But that's the way it works in California. This was us trying to get ahead of this problem before Bernie even announced. We knew it would be a huge detriment for Bernie Sanders, because we do really well with Latinos, young people, and independents. From a strategic point of view, it was a trifecta for us.

California was always going to be a very big deal to this campaign. It's a place Senator Bernie Sanders and Jane have real affection for. They understood the power of California. Even though we lost California in 2016 to Hillary Clinton, there were a lot of lessons learned about organizing effectively in the state.

Jeff wanted to develop strategies that made California a pillar of our campaign. We even considered California to be one of the first five: at headquarters, we talked about Iowa, New Hampshire, Nevada, and South Carolina — and then we would always include California. The state has an aggressive vote by mail program. Those ballots arrived at people's homes on the day of the Iowa caucuses.

Here's what people didn't know: we started California as early, and if not earlier, than we started the other four states. Now, what does that mean? I may be a consultant, but I just hate it when they say "we started here early" or "we focused on the community" or "we are taking this seriously." That's lovely — but tell me how much money you're spending, what resources you're allocating, and what you're talking about, because it sounds like you're trying to blow smoke up my dress.

I can tell you what we meant by it. We had staff on the ground in California, and were growing the operation at the same pace as Iowa. That's crazy if you think about it.

One sort of funny thing about California: Bernie has a lot of high-profile friends in the state. Everyone from heads of unions, to Hollywood types, to activists can email if they don't like what they're seeing on the ground. Their emails are then posed to you as, "What are we doing in California?" Stay tuned to see how we decided to tackle a gargantuan state.

What me and Jeff decided, very early on, was that we were going to treat California in many ways like it was six states. We called each of these subdivisions "areas." We had an area in San Diego; an area above that which included Orange County and the Inland Empire; then Los Angeles; the Central Valley and the Central Coast together; San Francisco; and, finally, Northern California. We had an area director in each one. We treated each of them like their own state. They each had their own field director, as well. In terms of pay scale, the area director was paid the same as state directors in other states. Same for area field directors. All the people we hired here were from the communities they led, and some of those people were true bad asses. For example, Jane Kim ran for mayor of freaking San Francisco. Now I had talked her into coming to work for us, to run that whole area.

On top of areas, we would have a statewide superstructure which would coordinate the activities of these six areas, and do some things that had to be done statewide. So we would have a state director, a deputy state director, a statewide field director, statewide communications, and statewide operations. In the very beginning, we were going to place political directors in each area. Partly for cost reasons, we decided to have two political directors, one in the north and one in the south. The California staff actually wanted three, which was not unreasonable in a state the size of California, but even a well-funded campaign has to make hard choices.

In the Summer of 2019, we were looking for someone who could coordinate statewide efforts in California, and help get the various areas up and running. We had lined up a state director. At the last minute, he ended up not being able to accept the job because of other commitments. We were left without a state director.

Luckily, we found Shelli Jackson, who came from Bakersfield and had run the most targeted State Assembly seat in California in 2018. She would serve as the top California person until a state director could be identified. We used a similar process in a number of states, including Iowa and New Hampshire.

We also moved the national deputy campaign manager, René Spellman. She had moved to Washington from Los Angeles, but still had an apartment there to go back and forth, to support Shelli with the entire state.

While staffing was coming along, we still had two problems.

A Quinnipiac poll released in mid-July of 2019 showed Latinos supported Bernie Sanders 25%, Joe Biden 23%, Kamala Harris 16%, and Elizabeth Warren 15%, which amounted to a statistical tie with Biden among Latinos. Bernie was also hyper-focused on California during that time. This poll and a couple others during that time in July led to an email from him to senior staff, just three days later.

"Jeff, Chuck, Faiz: Let's set up a meeting soon, perhaps this evening, with René and our top staff in California to talk about where we go from here in order to win the state," Bernie emailed on July 22. "Last few polls there have not been great."

He was also concerned because there was no state director, which was understandable.

What Bernie Sanders didn't know is that I had interviewed Rafael Návar to be the campaign manager, or the deputy campaign manager, or the political director. I wanted him to have a senior role in the campaign, because he was leaving Communication Workers of America in the Winter of 2018, and he was a brother from another mother. He's a true revolutionary. He's East Los Angeles, La Raza to the bone.

Long story short, I wanted him on the senior team, but he went back to California to run in a race against the CWA hierarchy. That's the sort of hilarious bad ass he is.

I wished him luck. I didn't want him to lose the election, but I knew if he did, he might become available in the summer. I really wanted Rafa, because I really trusted him. Ultimately, he came on board. Shelli became the deputy state director. We could not have won California without Shelli and without Rafa, and a whole host of amazing people who ran that state and each of the six areas.

We wanted to start opening up offices in the heart of the Latino community in all of these different areas, just as we did in East Las Vegas. Bernie was very much in favor of opening field offices in California, as was Jeff. Our Organizing Department was opposed because they were trying to run a more distributed program in California than me or Jeff or Bernie wanted. It became a bit of a sore point between the States Department and the Organizing Department, but eventually the California operation became much more independent of Organizing than what happened in most other states. The NPP program we ran was primarily done through the States Department with paid phones.

(Doing the NPP program with paid phones did reveal one very shocking truth. Paid phones to reach landlines were way more expensive to do with volunteers than with paid operators. It was because of the way our phone vendor was charging. Before the end of the campaign, I had developed an alternative source for distributed, volunteer phones that would have been a quarter of the price of what we paid. Even though we never got to use the new system on the campaign because the campaign ended, it has been tested in a bunch of places since. It works like a charm.)

We finally opened our first field office in East LA. We opened one in Coachella that César Chávez had literally used. We opened on the South Coast in Oxnard, where there had never been a presidential office. We ended up opening up 22 different offices and having over a hundred staff. Nobody not named Bloomberg even came close.

Even though there's a Bloomberg and his billions exception, none of the other campaigns came anywhere close to building the infrastructure that we built in this campaign, and no one did it as early as we did, directly in the community. This allowed us to knock on 1.6 million doors in the state. In a place as big as California, unfortunately, hitting just thousands of doors wasn't going to cut it.

As for the issue with NPP voters? We found out it was a universe of six million voters. Three million of them were automatic permanent absentee voters, which meant they weren't going to get a presidential ballot mailed to them with their normal ballot. There were bills moving through the state legislature to rectify this. Alex Padilla assured us they would send a presidential ballot to anybody who wanted one: they would receive postcards with the reminder, and they just had to ask for it.

Again, I was worried. It was an extra step for people to do, and we all know people are not going to take the time to request one. The governor ended up vetoing legislation that would have fixed this. That meant we had a huge problem walking into California.

Andrew Drechsler and his team at HaystaqDNA were our expert modelers for the campaign. They were joined by Asna Ansari, our California data director. What I needed them to do was create a list of the NPP voters who were most likely to be feeling the Bern.

We didn't have unlimited money for this project, so the six million NPPs immediately were halved to the three million permanent absentee voters. To find out who among those were most likely to be with us, our model came up with a workable universe of 500,000 of the most likely supporters, after tweaks. We did initially task our Organizing Department with reaching out to them through our distributed texting and distributed calling networks, asking them if they supported Bernie and connecting them with information to get the primary ballot.

It was an enormous undertaking. We began by getting people to re-register as Democrats and become a permanent absentee voter. As time went on, we had to change our strategy to get people just to request a ballot. We'd run out of time for the voter registration to change.

Bernie himself was strongly invested in the NPP voters. As the primary neared, he said so.

"It is critical that the voices of independents, of people who have no party preference, be heard," he said in February. "But many NPP voters do not know that they need to request a Democratic Party crossover ballot in order to participate."

We started knocking on voters' doors, asking them to request a ballot or change their registration, right there on our iPads. We were serving them digital ads. We were emailing them with a link to the site where they could request a ballot. We were also running Pandora ads to them. By now, you know it's a beloved platform of mine. If you clicked on the screen, it would take you to a site to request your ballot. We were even sending them pieces of mail that had the voter registration change card or the "request your ballot" card, where you just had to tear it off, fill it out, and send it in.

We also had one more crazy tool in our arsenal.

Some of the biggest users of my call centers — which, as I said, I used for Mexican redneck polls during the campaign — are nonprofits during off-cycles who want to put pressure on congressmen. UnidosUS, for example, may call you and say, "Your congressman is thinking of voting against the current immigration bill and we see you support immigration reform." My paid operators are trained to patch you directly through to your congressman for that chat. It's one of our biggest sellers.

I remember sitting in Jeff's office in the Fall. He said, "We just need to get more people to request a ballot." I replied, "Why don't we just call and ask them to and then we'll just patch them through to their county clerk in real-time?"

Jeff, being a good lawyer, said that first we should make sure the plan was legal. I mean, fair point Jeff — this is why they pay you the big bucks. So I checked with the lawyers. It was, in fact, legal. We called and, as long as they supported Bernie Sanders, we patched them through to request a ballot. If they weren't with us, I would just say, "Thank you, have a good day. I'm sorry to hear about your Raiders going to Las Vegas."

That's not all. We had a weekly call dedicated to NPP voters. What we were doing? What were the checks and balances? How many people had we identified? How many people have we patched through? How many people did we get to change their registration or request a ballot? This happened every week, for four months. How critical was this? There were people who didn't talk to their state directors in Iowa once a week, every damn week of the final month. That's how crazy in the weeds we were with organizing California.

In terms of the budget for the NPP program, I estimate we spent around $500,000 on outreach to these voters alone. Once people got their ballots in February, they could vote for a month before Super Tuesday. That final push was just getting people to send in their ballots, since we know who's got ballots and who hasn't sent it in. It just becomes a ground war at that point. Again, this is why infrastructure was so crucial.

Just like in Nevada, we were talking to Latinos. We were running ads in ethnic newspapers. For the first time, you had the Bloomberg effect making its presence felt. He was spending the most money of any politician in the history of California politics. That's saying a lot when we're talking about California! At one point, he was buying 3000 points of Los Angeles TV a week, which amounts to about $4 million a week in just LA.

He was saturating the airwaves. Friends of mine in California told me he hired hundreds, if not thousands, of paid operatives in the Inland Empire, and in LA, that were going door to door. He was paying money to everyone. Without Mike Bloomberg, we would have been the second-highest spender on TV in the state after Tom Steyer. As it was, we were third.

We ran tens of millions of dollars' worth of ads nationwide over the course of the campaign, all without an outside media consultant. Jeff Weaver wrote these ads, produced these ads, and we had a video team. Due to our financial advantage, we had a meeting about how we were able to go up on California TV. This was a huge difference compared to everybody else. As they were detailing when we were going to go up, and that the spend was going to amount to millions of dollars, I, of course, spoke up. I reinforced the importance of Spanish-language television.

While we were obviously going to do it, sometimes it's still important to allow your voice to be heard in moments like that. I took it upon myself to pull the media costs. I would figure out what it was going to cost to go up statewide in California in Spanish, at the same time we were going up in English, and stay up in Spanish the whole time.

In total, we ended up spending almost $3 million on Spanish-language TV in California. That's a big deal. I don't know of any presidential campaign in the history of presidential campaigns, before Mike Bloomberg, that had ever spent any kind of money like that in California. When you talk about why Bernie won California in convincing fashion, it had to do with lots of different layers of strategy.

In the end, we scaled up everything we had done in Iowa to be bigger in Nevada. We scaled it up again for this beautiful monstrosity that is California. In the late summer, when we went to California and weren't able to debut the immigration plan because of the El Paso tragedy, Bernie held a rally. He loves to come to California. The energy there is incredible.

If you looked at a lot of our rallies in places like Iowa and elsewhere, a lot of our audiences are young and white. Not so in California. They were always jam-packed with Latinos and people of color. Only weeks earlier, he had sent an email that he was concerned about California. That changed when we went to a

146

town hall meeting in a small community between Orange County and San Diego.

It was packed. There were people standing outside. They were all telling their stories, and it was all 100% Latinos. No presidential candidate had ever been to this community. I was waiting at Unidos to prep him. The first thing he said to me was, "Chuck, we had a really good event. The Latinos, they're really showing up. They're everywhere."

Just hearing that from Bernie Sanders is generally hilarious and amazing, but it was special, because of what it said about the energy behind his movement and the work we were putting in to get his voters out. You could just tell there was something really special happening.

What ended up happening? Bernie beat Biden 36% to 28%. Warren, who we had winning in an internal poll as late as September, came in third with 13%, followed by Bloomberg at 12%.

As for Latinos, Ben Tulchin's polling showed that we rose from 27% in early September, to 51% support according to the exit poll. It was a 24-point rise, with Biden's and Bloomberg's Latino support in the state both ending up in the teens.

In terms of our mad scientist focus on NPP voters, exit polls showed that we won half of independent voters in a multi-candidate race, which was outstanding. Biden received 18% support, and Bloomberg was at 14%. Again, we crushed it: we started early, spent money there, and layered in cultural competence.

Winning such a massive, critical state ended a journey that began improbably in December 2018. It started as I prepared to get on a flight to Cuba, but it ended on a competitive Super Tuesday, fueled by Latino voters.

Chapter 11

Back Home Again

The same day as the California primary, the primary was held in my home state, the Lone Star State. God, it felt good to be back home. In the back of my mind, I hear, "The stars at night are big and bright, clap, clap, clap, clap, deep in the heart of Texas." I told the story of starting my political career. I was working out of my beloved local union on a statewide race for Ann Richards. I was a lowly volunteer coordinator in East Texas, but I wore that with a great deal of pride. If you walk into my living room right now in Washington, DC, there are pictures of my grandkids — and there's a picture of me and Ann Richards. That was a special time in my life.

To go from being a Mexican redneck who lived in a trailer house, to helping run a presidential campaign with a group of amazing advisors, it felt like coming full circle in a fairy tale way. When the campaign began, I never thought in a million years that Bernie Sanders would be able to contend in Texas.

It was always in the back of my mind, what we would do, and how we would do it. But there were a couple popular Texans in the race, and one was Latino! I'm talking about Beto O'Rourke and Julián Castro, of course. I knew that Texas would always be a challenge, but I also knew from four years ago that we had a solid base of support in the state.

It's appropriate that California and Texas voted on the

same day, on Super Tuesday. Taken together, 42% of all Latino eligible voters reside in those two states. Let me back up the truck and repeat that: More than 4 in 10 Latino voters in the United States live in Texas and California. This matters for obvious reasons. You can't purport to care about Latinos, and ignore these two states, which never get any attention in the general election. There's historically been a lot of money thrown at voter registration in both states. That being said, there's never really been deep organizing or investment, because neither one of them have been a targeted battleground state for a presidential year.

As we were strategizing, I knew Latinos would have a major say in who won Texas. They're as big a portion of the vote in Texas as they are in California. The difference is that they vote at higher percentages in California, where they've invested in that community. Things like a $10 million English-only proposition had a hand in turning California blue forever. There's never been that direct investment into Texas.

I've been running races in Texas since I was a young man. I had hair, no gray beard, a big old chest, and a little waist. That's all gone now. It started in Dallas/Fort Worth in 1996, Houston was three months later, then Galveston, and then I ran four different races in San Antonio. One of those was for my dear friend Ciro Rodriguez, who was one of the first Latinos I ever worked for, in a special election in San Antonio back in 1997.

The election was triggered due to tragedy. Congressman Frank Tejeda died of brain cancer. It was a horrible thing. That led to a political free for all. Rodriguez was a young state representative at the time and a professor at the local community college, running in a super Democratic place on the South side of San Antonio. Every Mexican in San Antonio who had ever thought about running for Congress jumped into the race.

The AFL-CIO sent me down there, because I had just won a bunch of races in Texas. They said, "you run the labor program down there and mobilize all the labor union members to vote for Mr. Ciro Rodriguez because he's a good state rep who votes with labor 100% of the time." I'm like, "Shit, I get to go to San Antonio and eat Mexican food and go to Cowboys nightclub?" Needless to say, I was in.

It was the nineties, which means bare-knuckled Texas politics. While I remember some of it fondly, there was also negativity at times, like being bullied by another candidate's people. Ciro's wife was worried about her wellbeing, so one of my jobs back then was to drive her and his daughter home every night from the campaign office, like a bodyguard.

Ciro was so a raza, so Mexican, I would sit around and listen to him talk, talking about him and his brother riding their horses to the store to get cokes when they were little boys with money they earned from cutting sugarcane. I would just eat his stories up, like I was watching Bonanza on a Saturday night with my grand mama.

Fast forward to this Spring: his daughter Xochitl, the same one that I used to drive when she was a baby girl back then, is now 30 years old. She called me because I gave her a donation in her race for the state Senate in San Antonio. You know, it sucks to get old, but it's also really refreshing to see that there are good folks still carrying on a long lineage of good people running. Ciro Rodriguez was the most humble, unassuming politician I've ever been around.

That history in San Antonio would later come in handy. Bernie Sanders was holding his first big rally in the city at Cowboys Dance Hall. If I had a nickel for every piece of my boot that I had scraped off the bottom dancing on that floor, I'd be a rich man.

As we were watching the Texas primary develop, we didn't immediately start spending money. You can easily misuse $1 million because it's just such a big place. But then Beto, who entered the race with a bang, didn't last that long. Julián Castro ran as a strong progressive, but he never took off, either. I thought, if neither one of them is going to do anything, then we can be in this.

The main reason was this: if there's going to be 10 other people in this race, we're going to split the vote up. We estimated that 32% of the turnout would be Latino, so that was our opportunity. Of course, I had no idea of the consolidation that would happen before Super Tuesday, with the other moderate candidates rallying to Biden while Elizabeth Warren continued in the race. That was the game plan.

We started much later than in California. We knew it would be a much harder state. We weren't working with Mike Bloomberg money, but we still went directly into those communities with organizers on the ground, opened up offices, and ran a massive distributed program.

We had a young Latino brother named Chris Chu de León who was running the state for us. A big key was that we sent a bunch of staff from Iowa to Texas late, when we realized, man, we have a shot here. Leadership looked to me. I said I needed money to go up on Spanish TV in the Rio Grande Valley and in all the big markets. We took the Bernie Sanders immigration ad from Iowa. We ran it through the Valley to the tune of over $1 million worth of TV. It may not have been Bloomberg money, but I was trying to hold my own.

We started calling folks a little bit later than I would have liked, but a big part of the program in Texas was that they could start early voting two weeks before election day. This was before everybody consolidated behind Biden, so there were still seven or eight people in.

We were literally calling Latinos every day with paid operators in Spanish and English asking, "Are you with Tío Bernie? Oh, you are? Don't forget you can early vote. Let me tell you where your early voting location is." Then I was texting them all of that information as well. We spent hundreds of thousands of dollars on just calls and texts to get people to early vote. We ended up doing really well in the early vote numbers, because we were pounding the pavement to speak to Latinos.

At the end of the day, yes, I would've loved to spend $5 million to $6 million to mail every Latino and do as robust a program as we were able to do in other states. At the same time, none of us knew that everybody would drop out and get behind Joe Biden, while our leading progressive opponent would stay in. I also have polling that shows us winning Texas, and winning it fairly handily. We knew Latinos were with us, and the white vote was getting split up seven or eight ways, if the candidates hadn't gotten in line behind Biden. But I was still proud at the end of the day. I considered Texas a huge victory, even though we lost by a few points. We won the Latino vote yet again in another crucial state.

Bernie won Latinos 45% to 24% for Biden and 17% for Bloomberg, according to the exit poll. Ben Tulchin's internal polling showed Bernie's Latino support rising nearly 20% from December to election day.

Just for context: we spent a lot of money in Texas, but it was still less than 10% of what Bloomberg spent. This is just on Spanish communications that I could track alone. The lesson learned there is that you can move some Latinos by just spending lots of money.

I can confirm Bloomberg came to Texas. His people hired Latino consultants in the Valley, and spent $5 million in two months. There might be Mexicans in the Valley in Texas who now have two or three houses and who renamed their driveway, Michael Bloomberg Boulevard.

I was getting reports from my friends on the ground in the Valley who said, "I'm getting this money from Mike Bloomberg and I'm turning some people out, but you should know they're all voting for Bernie Sanders." I replied, "Sweet baby Jesus. Thank God." It took some of the pressure off.

The moral of that story: if you look at a map of Texas and the election results, Bernie Sanders won every single county along the border, many of which are heavily-Latino. Despite Beto O'Rourke and the power of his endorsement, we won El Paso County, as well.

Think back to where this story began in East Texas. I said my granddaddy papaw, who was only seven or eight years older than Bernie, reminds me a lot of him. Both were the hardest working older men I'd ever been around. What you see is what you get with them. When they spoke, people listened.

You would've never believed Bernie would have a chance to win Texas. But he had a great immigration policy, informed by a team of Latino and immigrant staffers. He championed Medicare for All. He invested in the community. I'm here to tell you that Texas can turn blue much quicker than people think it can. We proved it's possible.

Thinking about being back home, and coming full circle, I think of my little sister, Lisa Rocha Moore.

Many people judge the success of a parent on how their kids turn out. I would say my mother has been a huge success — not so much because of me, but because of my little sister. Much like me, she never went to college. Now, she is a very successful training manager for a company in Florida. She's just a huge success in my book. She actually gets to live on the water, and she owns a boat.

Like I said early on, adversity is what makes us who we are in the long run. My sister was just two-years-old when my dad left my mom. I've been raising her most of her life, acting as a big brother and father figure. I could not be more proud of the person she's become. I mention her here because, while Bernie's campaign was for a lot of people, it was most of all for people like Lisa. When he was talking to people all across America like my sister and my mother, he made it very clear to me why I dedicated all the time and effort to try to make him president. It would have directly affected my working-class family in the places where I come from.

It's safe to say that Super Tuesday didn't go exactly how we planned. I'd always wondered when everybody would rally around somebody, once they figured out we were fixing to win the nomination. We had internal polling that showed us winning every single Super Tuesday state, and even Florida a month out, with everyone in the race. Our polling was spot on in terms of the Bernie Sanders number in all those states, but our Biden number was wrong. Everybody dropped out. Biden had the moderate lane all to himself, while we had a progressive opponent spending $10 million on TV with a Super PAC.

Still, we did have other successful outreach to Latinos worth mentioning in the later states.

After Super Tuesday, we reallocated some resources. We doubled down in Arizona and Illinois because of how we had performed with Latinos. We were already up in Arizona with Spanish-language TV. We were also up with Spanish-language Pandora ads. We were sending four pieces of mail to Latinos attacking Donald Trump, and talking about our vision for Social Security and healthcare. Healthcare was a big issue for Latinos, as I outlined earlier.

This was the first time in the campaign where we were consistently attacked, with a focus on Latinos, for a prolonged period of time. I can tell you that every piece of our mail and Spanish-language content never attacked any other candidate. Yet, we got attacked in Arizona, Illinois and Florida by a super PAC supporting Biden, telling egregious lies that the campaign disavowed. That's neither here nor there. It did take something out of our base vote, because we weren't attacking anybody, and it did eat into our lead.

Regardless, we performed well with Latinos in Arizona, in part because our Nevada state director Sarah Michelsen was from there. It was always part of me and Jeff's strategic vision to move her and her best 20 organizers from Nevada right after caucus day, straight to her home turf, because she just knew the community so well.

You know, there's two sets of exit polls showing we won with Latinos in Arizona, and I prefer the one that's Sanders 41%, Biden 37%. Jokes aside, the UCLA data that they put out, in a deep dive into the precincts around Tucson, showed us winning the Latino vote pretty handily, and I'm proud of that.

We crushed it in Chicago with Latinos. We took organizers from Iowa, and moved them to the Windy City right after the Iowa caucuses. Latinos in the third-largest city in America love the senator from Vermont. A UCLA Latino Policy and Politics Initiative analysis found that in counties that were over 75% Latino, Bernie Sanders won 70% of the vote.

If there's one thing I hope this book has shown, it's how hard so many people worked to elect Bernie Sanders. His revolution lives on. But here's why I still take so much from even these latter states, where we lost, but still did very well with Latinos.

When I first started my firm, the first places that I knew would be looking to work with a brown consultant were the Latino nonprofits. The second was the Congressional Hispanic Caucus. I thought, if I can't get friends who I've literally helped get elected during my days in the union to hire me, I should just hang up my hat. Just how Latinos aren't a monolith, my God, our caucus is the furthest thing from a monolith.

There are a lot of super progressive people, and literally the most conservative Democratic member of Congress, all in the same caucus. I spent a lot of time working to elect Latinos to Congress, working with the caucus as far back as when it first started. Ciro Rodriguez in Texas would end up being chair of the Congressional Hispanic Caucus in my youth. When I started the firm, he was still in Congress, and they would figure out ways for me to work with them.

They started their first leadership PAC, and called it BOLD PAC. I was working with the leadership PAC back in the days when we were trying to raise $100,000 in one year. We thought that would be the most amazing thing ever. It went through several hands and several iterations. It's now run by one of my dearest confidants, Congressman Tony Cárdenas. He grew the success and influence of the PAC. They went from raising half a million or $1 million a year, to raising more than $10 million last cycle, becoming a powerhouse among the leadership PACs.

Now, I have been known to be quite the zealot when it comes to diversity and inclusion in all aspects of business, politics and, of course, campaign life. But my dirty little secret is that much of the time I'm just channeling Tony Cárdenas. I befriended Congressman Cárdenas shortly after he was first elected in 2013. I would soon find out we were kindred spirits, cut from the same cloth.

Tony grew up in a working-class family in California, I believe he's the youngest of a dozen kids or so. Tony has an engineering degree. He could be working in the private sector making millions of dollars, but he decided early on to devote his life to public policy. Tony wanted to give other Latinos and diverse communities a chance to climb the ladders of success. He is the rare example of a person in power who is always reaching down to pull people up with him.

If you're going to have a successful career in politics or consulting, you need mentors and brothers like Congressman Cárdenas. I'm lucky he has been there for me. Back when Scott Goodstein reached out to me to translate Bernie's website in 2015, I picked up the phone and called the congressman. I was looking to him for his opinion. Should I work for Bernie Sanders, or would I be punished like everybody else in the Democratic Party who was working against Hillary Clinton? Tony has openly talked about how he advised me to not only do the translation, but to get as much work as I possibly could, so I could learn from my experience. That's exactly what I did. That turned out to be one of the best decisions I ever made. One of the philosophies I live my life by is around the philosophy of chances and choices.

It's a big part of the way I look at life, especially through the lens of brown consultants. I have had many chances and I've made many choices — some of them good, some of them great, and some of them gosh darn awful. The key to success in this life revolves around the chances we get and the choices we make. You will notice throughout this book that there's one chance after another or one opportunity after another that I either take, or I decline. These are big turning points in my life. Having somebody to help guide you along the way as you're trying to build a business or break into politics is priceless. It's good to have people around you who channel the same way of life as you do. Tony has helped guide me along my path as only a few others have.

It turned out that Congressman Cárdenas gave us a heads up that the Hispanic Caucus was meeting with Joe Biden in the Fall, so we wouldn't be surprised. We ended up getting our invitation November 12.

We started looking at how much money Bernie had raised from each of their own constituents, which I thought was a really unique way to communicate with these members. You might be shocked to learn that Nydia Velázquez in New York has the most Bernie donors of any Congressional Hispanic Caucus member. I felt that was interesting as hell, and we had a great dialogue with her.

The meeting was in the evening, which I thought was horrible. Normally, the members do not hang out after votes. They all have fundraisers, dinners, and want to see their kids. I was being negative. I figured nobody would show up. I remember getting to the meeting, along with other Bernie staff. Congressman Cárdenas was there with three or four members. I texted Faiz. I heard Bernie was on the way. I figured Bernie would be tired, because he had a long day of meetings himself.

That's when more and more members started showing up. I was like, holy shit. It ended up being about 20 members. That is a big deal for the caucus. I went out the back door of the townhouse to go get Bernie. He seemed like he was shocked to see me.

"Chuck, how you doing?" Bernie said. "I haven't seen you in a while."

In the interest of full disclosure for the younger staffers of color reading this, sometimes you feel some type of way. It can rear its head even when you get older. I knew deep down that Bernie knew how hard I was working, even though he didn't see me everyday. It still gave me a momentary sinking feeling in my belly. I also knew he meant no harm. We went inside.

Bernie gave his remarks. Faiz and I sat off to the side. They started going around the room for every member to ask a question. Congresswoman Nanette Barragán went first.

"I'm going to get to my question," she said to Bernie. "But I just want you to know that I would not be in Congress if it wasn't for Chuck Rocha. You were smart to hire him." Then she turned and pointed at me. It caught me off guard. I remember tears welling up in my eyes.

I worked on her very first race. She fired her consultants after her primary, and then she got into a runoff. We knew each other from BOLD PAC, she hired me, and we won. It was historic. She had never run for office before, other than being a city councilwoman.

Ruben Gallego was with Biden, but he talked to Bernie about the work I was doing and why it mattered. We did not have a single Hispanic Caucus member who was with us at that point in time, but they wanted to let Bernie know they saw what was happening with his commitment to Latinos.

The most heartwarming one, the one that really put it over the top, was Ben Ray Luján. He was running for Senate, but had showed up at a Congressional Hispanic Caucus BOLD PAC meeting. Keep in mind that for the last two cycles, he had been running the DCCC, but after the meeting he would tell me he showed up just because I was going to be there.

"I'm proud to have chaired the DCCC in the last cycle and I'm also proud to have brought on Chuck Rocha as one of our consultants," he said. "He worked on 32 of our winning Congressional races and he also helped us write our outreach to Latinos and all of our multiracial outreach." He went on and on, concluding his remarks by saying, "the smartest thing you ever did as a campaign was make him a senior part of your leadership team."

I felt so guilty about getting all of this praise. I remember on my Uber ride home sending Faiz a text saying, "Look, I know that meeting looked like it was set up to be a Chuck Rocha love-fest, but I swear to God I had no idea that anybody was going to say a damn thing."

It was also very surreal. This was in November, in the heat of the campaign fight: it was the peak of pressure, as I worried about Nevada, as I worried about everything. But it was a moment to step back and think: maybe I'm actually doing something bigger than what I think I'm doing here. Maybe my presence on this campaign means way more than I'm giving myself credit for. I had never really taken the time to stop and think about it.

I don't want to have a whole bunch of people singing my praises or putting my name in a marquee. I do want there to be ten more Solidarity Strategies in ten years when I leave. That was when it hit me that what we were doing was really special. It had been noticed by the people that I loved the most. I'll never forget that.

Chapter 12

In Solidarity:
Where We Go From Here

Joe Biden, and a lot of Democratic candidates for that matter, don't surround themselves with senior Latino operatives, like Bernie did on those car rides. Beyond just the access part of it, it's also about influence.

I talked a lot of crap about establishment consultants in this book. Look, things like the closing ad we did in Iowa and Nevada and elsewhere — that tie all of the cultural competency lessons from this book together — don't happen in most campaigns. For folks outside of politics, it may sound like common sense. Like, why wouldn't people do this? It's important to understand that it's the exception, and not the rule.

There are plenty of consultants who are my friends. Some of them are good. None of them mean any harm. But they've been taught how to do things one way, and there's more than one way to do it — as the Bernie Sanders campaign proved. You can do it this way now.

I took the responsibility of running the pilot program to do every angle of it, to show that it's possible. You don't have to have a focus group and a poll, message testing or ad testing, and all this shit that you think you have to have to run a campaign. Sometimes, if you'll just simply take the time and spend the money to ask voters what resonates with their community, and have Latinos up and down the organization, people will show up and vote for you.

In the future, if anybody wants to brag about their Latino operation with some catch-all like "we have deep ties to the community" or "great endorsers," stop them right there. All of that is meaningless rhetoric.

Ask some simple questions: How many Latinos work on your campaign? How many of those are in leadership positions and have budget authority? How much money are you going to spend on the Latinos compared to the general market, AKA white people? How early are you going to start? These are some important questions to see if somebody is actually running a program to any constituency — not just Latinos, but to Native Americans, to black people, to any of the folks who are not what people think of as the general audience.

Messaging matters. Is it the most important thing? I would argue it's equally as important as taking the time to go speak to somebody who normally doesn't vote. We spent a lot of time talking to Latinos who never get asked anything. They're newly registered, they're an infrequent voter, or maybe they never caucused before. It started with the strategy around the targeting of Latinos, followed swiftly thereafter by the messaging piece.

Of course, we had a strong messenger. Bernie stays on message no matter what the hell he's talking about. He's going to talk about Medicare for All, he's going to talk about forgiving college debt and free community college, a $15/hour living wage, the Green New Deal, and guess what? Latinos love all of that. You still have to take the time and effort to go talk to them about that, though.

I get upset when people put all this work into their endorsement lists to blast out to their press list, as if, boom, we can check off Latino outreach now. Time to go drink a refreshing LaCroix. That's cool that a Latino city councilman or congresswoman endorsed you, but if a tree falls in the woods and no one hears it, did it make a sound?

What I mean by that is that endorsements really don't matter for the most part, unless you're going to put money behind those endorsements. If you put that congresswoman's name on a mail piece or a radio ad, if you go spend a couple of hundred thousand dollars to tell the Latino community that this Latino validates this campaign and is standing with us, then that endorsement means something.

The first three months of the Latino operation, we had no polling, but we had cultural competency. If this book was called "The Mexican Redneck and His Long List of Flaws," it would be much longer and less interesting. What I did bring to the campaign was 30 years of experience, including helping to win back over 30 congressional seats, in places where Latinos were over 20% of the electorate most of the time. So I had some idea what to do. You don't have to have polling to make it perfect. Don't let perfect be the enemy of good.

Next, sweet baby Jesus, start early. It sends a signal that you give a shit about us.

You should start reaching out to people of color at the same time you start reaching out to white voters in any campaign when you're financially able to do it. Not as window dressing. Not siloed off from everybody else. With the same vigor and know how that you do everything else.

For example, the complicated and really layered communications we ran to Latinos — guess what? It's the same operation the regular consultants are running to the targeted white woman who lives in the Philadelphia suburbs, starting in June before that next year's election, because they prioritize her. Funny how that works, right? It's the same as the white male factory worker who voted for Barack Obama, but then four years later voted for Donald Trump. They start spending money on that dude really early on, often to persuade them. Well, if you start doing that with Latinos, you'll get the same kind of turnout. That's why early investment is just so crucial.

Lastly, you have to have people from the community doing this work.

You constantly hear me say brown consultants matter. If it sounds similar to Black Lives Matter, let me just take a moment to say unequivocally that Black lives do fucking matter. It's more important now than ever before to say we stand with our Black brothers and sisters after the killings of Ahmaud Arbery, Breonna Taylor, and George Floyd. I love that movement, and I mean no disrespect when I talk about brown consultants.

This is my effort to spotlight not just brown, but also Black people, in the only industry in America that's more white than Congress, and more white than any other profession in the country — political consulting. It really is a good old boys network. People hand each other work all day long. What you lose is that cultural competency. It's also important to remember that Bernie Sanders didn't hire Chuck Rocha to be a brown consultant.

He hired me to be a consultant; I just happened to be Latino. Probably 20% of my overall work was making sure that this program was fully funded and run in the most robust way. The other 80% of my time was doing outreach to all voters via regular mail, radio, and door to door campaigns. I'm proud to talk about the Latino program, but don't just pigeonhole brown people into just doing work for Latinos. Every Latino that worked on this worked in another department that was not Latino-focused.

That's the crux and the backbone of the success we had. There's also the multilayered paid program we ran that we detailed in Nevada, which brings nuance into reaching a community that is younger and older, speaks English and Spanish, and might be reached on Spanish-language radio or on Pandora. Don't just put up a Google-translated ad on Univision. That shit don't fly anymore, and you will get called out in this media environment.

Bernie Sanders had the right message, but he's not perfect. No one is. Work had to be done to spread his message and tie him to the community. We took the time and energy to do that. We proved that if you build it, they will come.

I talked about how big an impact the endorsement from Congresswoman Alexandria Ocasio-Cortez had on this campaign, and how for the first time I saw a congressional endorsement really, really matter. Her loyalty to a man who I love showed the true character of who she is, and that she was reflective of this movement.

The big rally in New York was historic, and a shot in the arm for our momentum. What people don't know is that she came to headquarters and recorded video ads for us. She recorded TV commercials for us. She did them in English, and she did them in Spanish. Then we put those out and delivered those to Latinos in Iowa, and in Nevada. What's incredible about AOC is that she was moving young white kids as much as she was moving Latinos. She was just a great messenger.

I tried to explain this to a reporter one time, that Latinos are a very aspirational community. We're way younger than the general population, but we're aspirational. We know that if the government can provide a net benefit rather than be an obstacle, there's no doubt we're going to work hard enough to achieve our dreams. We're going to work two or three jobs. We're going to outwork everybody.

Every time an abuela or a young Latino saw AOC on a mail piece or a TV ad, they saw her as their daughter, their grand-daughter, their sister, and it showed what was possible for their own children to be. Much in the same way people talked about the impact of Tiger Woods on young Black kids when he first showed up on the scene, the idea was if this young Latina could be a member of Congress, then my daughter could be, too.

She was a big influence on our operation in Iowa and Nevada. We put the money and the talent and the cultural competency behind her message, to deliver that directly to Latinos and to overall voters through digital ads and all the other means at our disposal. It was a central piece of our strategy, because she was such a good validator for Bernie Sanders.

On a personal note, sometimes you see that when young people pull off something like she did in New York City, a lot of people would have won that race and become super cocky. Maybe some people would have revealed things that didn't fall in line with the values of the movement or Bernie Sanders.

But AOC lived her values.

There's a whole generation of young Latinos, who have come of age, graduated college, and are raising families. They lived through the pandemic and were worried about their mothers or their jobs, and now have lived with this racial strife and police brutality epidemic. It really brings to light what the revolution was always about. They really align ideologically with AOC.

As a 78-year-old senator's campaign for president comes to an end, there have to be people out there who will pick up that mantle, our values and continue the fight. It would be unfair to put it all on her, but she is a leader now and in the future. It's important to mention that.

The campaign came up a little bit short. You don't win every battle, and I've lost a lot more elections than I've won. I created Nuestro PAC after the campaign, so never again in my lifetime will a donor come to me because of what I did for Bernie Sanders without an avenue to invest in the work. I will take that money and put it right back in the community, to turn out Latinos and voters to make sure that there's a progressive agenda in this country that represents the values of Bernie Sanders, me, and working Americans all throughout the country.

The biggest difference is that Congress doesn't always represent people. People are hurting. The economy is faltering, and people have no money. This is the most pivotal time in American history, and I want to do my part.

Stephanie Valencia, one of the top Latina leaders in the country, holds a private Latino leadership meeting that happens once a quarter to share ideas and values. I went to the Summer 2019 meeting. It had every brown leader there from groups like Center for Popular Democracy, Mijente, Justice Democrats, Indivisible, and Alliance for Youth Action.

They invited senior leadership from every campaign to come to Vegas in a private setting. You had to do a round robin with seven or eight different Latino leaders, who were sent in different rooms around different issue sets. One room might be about hiring Latinos and diversity, another about how the campaign is dealing with pay equity, and yet another on immigration policy. They put you through the ringer. It's super intimidating and super hard for any campaign, right?

For every question they had, I had the right answer, because of the work we outlined earlier. When they talked about hiring, boom. Nailed it. When they talked about pay equity, boom. Nailed it. When they talked about immigration, I could talk about immigrants coming together to write policy recommendations. How are you prioritizing our community? We already have a budget. We're spending money. Our first communication in Iowa is in Spanish. Every time they threw me a pitch, I would just turn around, and yank it over the right field wall.

I called Jeff after. I told him it was one of the proudest moments of the campaign.

It wasn't because the people from other campaigns weren't great. It was because they really weren't in a leadership position. That's something you find out quickly when the questions are coming fast and furious.

This key concept would rear its head again as the campaign wound down.

I received a lot of congratulations and well-wishes during that time from my peers and fellow staffers. Basilisa Alonso damn near made me cry for "holding the door open for Latinos" after I got my opportunity, which she said gave so many of them "the chance of a lifetime" to work for Bernie. I also got a message from Kristian Ramos, a sharp consultant who, like many of us, understands the power of courting Latinos and the danger for Democrats when the work isn't done.

"I did what you would have done if you were running a campaign," I told him.

People knew these fights in electoral politics were not new, and that I was doing what we've all talked about, what we've all said we wanted to do in meetings like the one Stephanie Valencia created.

I will always lift up Tim Tagaris. He raised an unbelievable amount of money and is a brilliant architect of the fundraising machine for Bernie, along with digital fundraising director Robin Curran. But I know great people that worked for Kamala, that worked for Joe Biden, and really good people that worked for Elizabeth Warren. They didn't have the same amount of money, but I know they would have had the same philosophy as I had, if they'd been given my seniority and influence in their campaign to make decisions about its structure. I just know because they're my brothers and my sisters. I believe that from the bottom of my heart.

At the end of the day, I could take my tools and cry and go home. I'm going to stay in this fight. I launched Nuestro PAC, and I'm going to take the lessons I learned here with me. I'm going to tell people they don't have to be scared to talk about Medicare for All, or college affordability, or a living wage. We're going to talk about it. We're going to be proud to talk about it.

One final thing. I didn't take the campaign manager role this time. I'm not thinking about any type of senior role in future campaigns. I am looking forward to 2022 and 2024 and beyond in one respect, though.

The incredible young brown people that grew into their roles this time, will now be able to have more senior roles for future races and presidential cycles. We created a pipeline. If there's anything I'm most proud of, it's strengthening the Democratic Party for years to come with amazing young Latinos.

There's no other way to describe it: not me. Us. It was their work that put us in position to build a multi-racial coalition.

Belén's work, and Analilia's work, and Luis's work.

It was Faiz and Ari, but also Arianna, John, Becca, and Senator Turner.

It was Jeff Weaver. Thank you my brother.

Above all, it was the man whose message, commitment, and investment inspired millions of Latinos, changing the political calculation forever.

Tío Bernie.

Acknowledgments

I want to thank Adrian Carrasquillo who was my collaborator and editor for this book. I also want to acknowledge my Solidarity Strategies staff who helped me bring this book to life, kept the firm running and managed our clients. They acted as my agents, promotional team and support group. I love you all: Luis Alcauter, Eileen Garcia, Daysi Gonzalez and Joseline Garcia.

I want to thank my family for all the love and support that they have given me over the years. My mother Sandra Bussell, my sister Lisa Moore, her husband and my fishing partner Cliff Moore, and their kids Kaydra, Kutter and Kai. I also want to give a special shout out to my son Charles A. Rocha and my 2 beautiful grandsons, the Rocha Boys themselves, Wyatt and Rowan Rocha.

Relationships are hard enough without trying to have one while running a presidential campaign. Ebony Ivory Payne, my rock, my council, my therapist and, most importantly, the love of my life: thank you for putting up with all this craziness and still loving me.

I want to thank the entire Bernie 2020 staff, especially Amanda Arias who kept Jeff Weaver's and my schedule and life together during some of the craziest periods in our lives. I did not have the space or the memory to list everyone on this campaign who touched my life, but know that each of you changed my life forever and I am very proud to have fought side by side with you to try to elect Sen. Bernie Sanders.

And to you Senator Sanders: I saved the most important acknowledgement for you. I would not be where I am today without the opportunity that you gave me and my firm. I don't take any of this for granted and I am so thankful to be one of your advisors. You and your wife, Dr. Jane Sanders, have always treated me with respect and opened your home to me. I wrote in this book that you remind me of my Papaw and all I can say is that I have never loved or respected anyone in my life as much as I respected him and my Mamaw. Thank you.

I dedicate this book to my Mamaw, Evelyne Bussel, Papaw, CJ Bussell, and my father, Ed Rocha, who are all no longer with us. I also dedicate this book to my mother, Sandra Bussell. They made it possible for me to be here right now in this moment. I love you all.

Special Thanks to Bernie 2020 Latinx Staff

Ana Acosta
Ivan Aguilar
Luis Alcauter
Candida Alfaro
Jacob Allen
Basilisa Alonso Mendoza
Marya Alvarado
Violeta Alvarez
Nicholas Amadeo
Daniel Andalon
Sheila Angelo
Brianna Arduca
Amanda Arias
Ector Arreola
Joseph Aszterbaum
Manuel Ayala
Suze Banasik
Resa Barillas
Luca Barton
Nelsy Batista
Laura Becerra
Emma Bertrand
Tanner Bierstedt
Christian Bolanos
Rocio Bolivar
Cruz Bonlarron

Daniel Bravo
Jessica Bravo
Marco Briones
Steven Buitron
Deisy Cabrera
Rivan Calderin
Omar Camacho
Jonathan Campo
Jorge Castaneda
Jesus Castillo-Camargo
Julian Cepeda
Bryan Cervantes
Susana Cervantes
Maria Chapa
Bobbi Jo Chavarria
Chris Chu de León
Vicente Cortez
Antonio Cruz
Socrates Cruz
Marco Cruz Blanco
Ariadna Davis
Elena De La Cancela
Gabriel de la Cerda
Patricia De La Hoya
Jazmin Devora
Neidi Dominguez

Rebecca Dominguez
Edin Enamorado
Michael Enriquez
Estefania Espinosa
Salvador Espinoza
Joze Estrada
Mario Fernandez
Leda Fisher
Valerie Flanagan
Nathali Flores
Victoria Flores
Isaac Flores-Huerta
Maria Florian Arriaga
Joshua Gacita
Jose Galarza
Jaime Gallardo
Connor Gallivan
José Gaona
Eileen Garcia
Osvaldo Garcia
Joseline Garcia
Darla Garcia
Daniel Garcia
Morgane Garnier
Jocelyn Garduno
Millan Gledhill
Ernesto Gloria
America Gomez
Sydney Gonzales
Roxanna Gracia
Angelo Greco
Vanessa Grisko
Juan Guerra
Jacqueline Guzman
Leonel Hechevarria
Coa Heiden

Stephanie Hernandez
Martin Hernandez
Joese Hernandez
Jessica Hernandez-Cruz
Oliver Hidalgo-Wohlleben
Janet Hurtado
Alejandro Jacquez
Mahalia Jaramillo
Diego Jauregui
Issis Juliao
Kimberly Juliao
Thomas Kennedy
Elizabeth Lira
Leticia Lopez-Sanchez
Judas Marcial
Jose Mariscal-Cruz
Bianca Marquez
Nesler Martinez
Rito Maxtla
Celina Medina
Eric Medina
Miguel Medrano
Annaly Medrano
Analilia Mejia
Angel Melendez
Reyna Mercado Vargas
Anna Mesa
Melissa Michelson
Alexandre Monnier
Natalie Monteiro
Robert Moreno-Elizalde
Rafael Návar
Tanya Navarro
Anabel Nevarez
D'Angelo Oberto-Besso
Angel Obeso-Ferracin

Michael Ortiz
Oscar Ortiz
Maria Palacios-Trujillo
William Parada
Sandra Peeters
Laura Pelner
Scarlet Peralta
Angelo Perlera
Francesca Petrucci
Crystal Quevedo
Anthony Ramirez
KJathy Ramirez
Michael Ramirez
Marcela Ramirez-Wagner
Andres Ramos
Alexandria Ramos - O'Casey
Tomás Rebecchi
Bianca Ixara Recto
Jaqueline Reynoso Marquez
Hector Rios Diaz
Leticia Rios
Antonia Rivera Hernandez
Thomas Rocha
Joshua Rodriguez
Matthew Rodriguez
Ellyana Rodriguez
Alexa Rodriguez
Arianne Rodriguez
Nelson Rodriguez
Nora Rodriguez
Aidan Rodriguez Swanson
Carlos Rojas Rodriguez
Marcial Romero
Naomi Roochnik
Claudia Ruano
Gabriel Saldana

Brandon Sanchez
Luis Sanchez-Conde
Ivan Sandoval
David Santillan
Julia Santos
Gabriel Silva
Maria Belén Sisa
Aylin Soto
Jacquelyn Spicer
Samuel Sukaton
Anahi Tapia Torres
Lawrence Thompson
Brandy Tinoco-Garcia
Mary Torres Cardona
Allison Tovar
Joseph Traina
Katherine Ulloa
Vanessa Umana
Daniela Valencia
Victor Valladares
Luis Vasquez
Chris Vega
Andrea Vega
Krystal Velez
Juliette-Cyré Velez
Jenna Vella
Jorrel Verella
Jose Villalobos
Angelica Villaneda
Jaedon Villasista
Hudson Villeneuve
Angel Vizcaino
Stephanie Campanha-Wheaton
Jose Zayas Caban

CPSIA information can be obtained
at www.ICGtesting.com
Printed in the USA
BVHW030222100221
599790BV00009B/169